Writing the Land:
Windblown I

Writing the Land: Windblown I

Edited by Lis McLoughlin, PhD

Published by
NatureCulture LLC
Northfield, MA

Looking Down
    North Fork, Coeur d'Alene
by Robert Wrigley

Two hundred feet above the river,
we sheltered under a single poncho.
The downpour came hard on the trail

for ten soaking minutes, then stopped,
and sun reappeared and a rainbow
plunged a leg directly into the water.

From a quarter mile away we could see,
all the way to the hole's bottom
the seven primal shades of light,

like a great illuminated hoof on a boulder,
through which trout drifted and swam,
like motes in the river's shimmering blue eye.

Photo: Connecticut River Rocks by Marty Espinola

Foreword

At its heart, conservation is an act of grace, an act of saving the more-than-just-human world. It is a human act, one that we are called to for any number of reasons, be it concern for self-preservation, a sense of responsibility, or a love of the warp and weft in the tapestry of life. While conservation strategies cannot succeed unless grounded in the realities of ecology and genetics, few, if any, conservationists dedicate their lives to its practice simply out of scientific curiosity. This is perhaps why we imagine conservation to take place across "landscapes," a concept that evokes deeper emotional imagery than "ecosystems" or "biomes." Envisioning landscapes evokes imagery that encompasses the life found there as well human engagement with it.

Conservation on the scale of landscapes takes many forms. Here in the United States, the forms that comes quickly to mind are the iconic parks and wilderness areas owned in the public trust and managed by government agencies at the federal or state levels – as examples, Great Smoky Mountains National Park, Bob Marshall Wilderness, and Adirondack Park. But as large as such ecological reserves are, even collectively they are insufficient to achieve the full scope of what is needed to ensure the integrity of the natural world throughout the country. Gaps in protection abound.

Fortunately, conservation practice does not rely solely on public ownership and management of lands and waters. Conservation on private lands, most notably here by land trusts, is critical in creating a more comprehensive approach to promoting long-term ecological integrity. The ability of land trusts to focus on small but ecologically important lands and waters, work with landowners to achieve diverse but complementary goals, and create natural areas embedded within regions more heavily modified by human transformation, makes them an indispensable part of the conservation tool kit.

And it is also within land trusts that we can see, by the words and actions of those involved with them, love of the more-than-just-human world. Call it by any name you like – environmental ethics, nature appreciation, biophilia – those involved with land trusts evince a deep respect for what they hope their work will conserve. And that respect, that love, easily expands beyond each person's internal environment, their innermost thoughts and feelings. It readily emerges into what they share with others in conversation and in writing.

While the connection between land conservation and poetry may at first seem incongruous, it is anything but. The poetry of Robinson Jeffers, Gary Snyder, and Mary Oliver among many others exemplify the enduring strength of such a connection, linking what is seen and experienced amidst the natural world – what is felt in our bones as we engage with the lives and landscapes of others not like ourselves – with an understanding of its inherent value. The poetry found here in this volume takes this connection one step further, linking this understanding to specific places. Places that are loved for what they are, full of grace.

---Stephen C. Trombulak, Ph.D.
Professor Emeritus of Biology and Environmental Studies
Middlebury College, Middlebury, VT
30 July 2022

Introduction

The wind knows no borders...

Land and poems adapt as you move across the continent. In the east, where I am from, we notice change writ across the land by nature and by humans who are part of nature; about forests that were fields and then forests again, and boundaries of stone and water, the edges, the details.

In the midwest they don't often write about fences, but instead their eyes focus on the timeless vastness of sky and earth——the spaces, the eternal work of weather, of the elements——water, earth, wind, fire——of generations.

And on the west coast, there is a mix of these——as if each poem had made its own journey, picking up elements of its identity along the way, remaking itself as it goes.

Let these poems about lands which have been safely conserved for the future, transport you too. Feel the excitement of travel the way a seed might, wondering what was ahead, looking for a home, at the mercy of the wind.

——-L. McLoughlin
May 2022

Photo: Milkweed Fibers by Marty Espinola

TABLE OF CONTENTS

I. JEFFERSON LAND TRUST (Washington) 1
  -Valley View Forest-Agodon 2

II. INLAND NORTHWEST LAND CONSERVANCY (Washington)19
  -Coeur d'Alene River-Barnes and Wrigley.................................24
  -Palisades Park-Lee..28
  -Waikiki Springs Nature Preserve-Merino.................................31

III. KANSAS LAND TRUST (Kansas)...37
  -Wells Farm-Mirriam-Goldberg 38
  -Prairiewood-Brimhall 46

IV. THE NATURE CONSERVANCY (Kansas).................................55
  -Flint Hills-Low 56

V. VERMONT LAND TRUST (Vermont)...73
  -East Montpelier Trails-LoVasco...74
  -Knoll Farm-Day...79
  -Charlotte Park and Wildlife Refuge-Close 84

VI. HILLTOWN LAND TRUST (Massachusetts)...........................91
  -Conwell Property-Lin..92

VII. PECONIC LAND TRUST (New York)..................................... 109
  -Reel Point-Landau... 112
  -Bridge Gardens-Landau... 116
  -Smith Corner Preserve-Chaskey.. 121
  -Quail Hill Farm-Chaskey 122

VIII. BRANFORD LAND TRUST (Connecticut) 127
  -Beacon Hill-Peterson.. 128

IX. CAPITAL REGION LAND CONSERVANCY (Virginia)............ 147
-Verina LandLab at Deep Bottom-Scott 151
-Warwick Road-Moses... 154
-James River Park System-Lee.. 156
-Malverne Hill Farm-Wegener.. 160

X. PROSPECT PARK (New York City)...................................... 165
-Poets: Opalanietet, Parker, and Picaro

XI. FLUSHING MEADOWS CORONA PARK (New York City)..... 183
-Poets: Acosta and Hahn

-Poets' Biographies.. 204
-Artists', Essayists', and Translators' Biographies 209

JEFFERSON LAND TRUST

Washington

Jefferson Land Trust is a private, non-profit, community-driven conservation organization in Jefferson County, located on the stunning Olympic Peninsula in Washington State. We work with the community to preserve the iconic open space, working lands and habitat of this special place.

In Jefferson County, our livelihoods and way of life depend on the health of our water, forests and farmland. We all have a stake in this land, which is why Jefferson Land Trust works to bring people with diverse perspectives together to collaborate and find creative solutions and common ground.

From protecting habitat for wildlife, to facilitating the generational transfer of land, to supporting our agriculture, we work with landowners, farmers, government agencies, the timber industry, the Navy, local schools, scientists, artists, volunteers, and many more community groups and community members on a range of projects for the benefit of all those who live in and visit this special region — now and into the future.

-Valley View Forest—Kelli Russell Agodon

Valley View Forest

In the 65-acre Valley View Forest, western red cedar and Douglas fir combine with bigleaf maple, sword fern, and huckleberry to create a thriving, dynamic landscape. The lush understory provides critical habitat for local wildlife, including coyote, Columbia black-tailed deer, and bobcat; and the forest offers refuge to a variety of birds. Tributaries that feed the west fork of Chimacum Creek flow through the forest on their way to the vibrant agricultural valley floor below, where Jefferson Land Trust has worked with many local landowners and a host of partners to protect farmland and creek-side properties, as well as to restore habitat for endangered salmon. Human visitors enjoy public trails here.

Our long-term vision for Valley View Forest is to combine it with the larger, adjacent Chimacum Ridge Forest when we purchase those 853 acres in 2023. Eventually, Valley View Forest will serve as the entrance to a vibrant working community forest with recreation and education opportunities. We seek to manage the forest in a way that provides long-term economic, cultural, and social benefits, and supports a rich diversity of species, and we are involving the wider community in decision-making and planning.

All Valley View Forest photos by Tim Lawson

Gateway to Valley View
by Kelli Russell Agodon

As you arrive, thank the blankets
of moss, the bedroom of fallen leaves,
the smallest creatures who see big leaf maples
as rooftops to their homes. As you arrive,

let the Douglas fir remove any heavy coats
patched with sorrow, turn off the newscasts
repeating in your mind.

The forest speaks to you
in whispers of branches, of wingspan
and feathers the color of sky.

Open the door to the sunlight that rains
lightdrops, to the mist that holds your hand.

Before you leave, clean the fog
from your fingernails and sweep the wind
off the trail. Before you leave, speak

to the snowberries and ask
their proper name—*Symphoricarpos,* they whisper
as you wash the soil from your skin,

wipe the dew from your eyes. Before you leave,
follow the fern pathway back to your life
and thank the daybirds for always remembering
there are so many songs of joy.

Love Song to Valley View
by Kelli Russell Agodon

Welcome dear guests of this forest. Walk gently
like clouds that hold us near. See the light
catch the swornferns and reach toward sky
while staying on the path. Praise the uplands,
the farmlands, the salmon of Chimacum Creek.
How lucky we are to have each other. Nature heals.
If we quiet, we hear this world speaks to us
in sweet whispers. Honor the woods,
step softly onto this sacred land.

Song of the Spring
by Kelli Russell Agodon

In the forest, the voice of god
is a treefrog, an evening chorus
reminding us it is spring. We believe
we are alone here, but we are followed
by chickadees, the dirt we carry on our shoes.
Because our hearts are shopping carts, we fill
with them with mossy rocks and messy-headed
fern—we know the forest soothes. And
when a chipmunk rushes past us and scribbles
I find peace in the chaos on a big leaf maple,
we know we have found our home. If god
is a treefrog, let her find love at a rowdy party,
noise-cancelling lungs, let's hold hands
we walk deep into the forest, all this harmony
to breathe and breathe and breathe.

Magic Wand(erers)
by Kelli Russell Agodon

All week we discussed
magic, how we heard a gust
of traffic, a few farm animals

across the road. Until we didn't.
Until the moss-covered trees
covered our ears with their branches.

Until a treefrog sang a solo.
All week, swordferns forgot
the sharpness of their name

and waved hello in a breeze.
Because the sky is tender,
it reminds us to walk softly

on provided paths
while our stresses disappear.
Magic. Who would have thought

we didn't need someone to say,
Abracadabra or *For my next trick*.
Watch the leaves change color

and tumble down. All week,
we whispered: *Magic*. We almost
didn't believe our eyes.

Chasing Light at Valley View
by Kelli Russell Agodon

Listen. The lichen
whisper to the humans
who pause
as swordfern sparkle

with sun. The maple tree
without leaves is a poet
empty of words. Trust her.
It's impossible to know

if the ferns will punctuate the trail
or if the trail is a run-on sentence
bluejays keep trying to correct.
How can a poem live in a forest?

How can life be covered in moss?
Listen. The spring birds return
and they dress in a wingspan
of clouds. There is a legend

that at believes an owl's song
can lead a poet straight
to the light we are all trying
to hold. Sometimes the quiet,

the lichen gets lost in the poem
like when we turned left
instead of right, but dear one,
in this forest we are never lost.

INLAND NORTHWEST LAND CONSERVANCY

Washington

Our mission

To conserve, care for, and connect with lands and waters essential to life in the Inland Northwest.

Our vision

We envision a future of interconnected natural habitats throughout the Inland Northwest, supporting thriving populations of native plants and wildlife, respected, and enjoyed by all who call this region home.

Serving Eastern Washington and North Idaho since 1991

-Coeur d'Alene River—Kim Barnes and Robert Wrigley
-Palisades Park—DJ Lee
-Waikiki Springs Nature Preserve—Maiah A Merino

Transitions
by Heidi Lasher

High in the Bitterroots, the St. Joe River spans the width of a long stride, then a hop, now a fallen Douglas Fir. In summer, a boy stands waist-deep in the lower river, holding a fly rod high in the air. Yellow filament makes a cursive figure-eight, landing soft hackle on the surface, a tasty morsel hiding a tiny brass hook. Below him, the river pools into a giant lake. Here the mountains kneel and basalt that once spilled from earth's molten center pokes skyward.

I am standing on one such rock, between highland and lowland, larch forests and desert scrub, batholith and sand. To the west, flood-exposed rock and rubble mark a scar that rips diagonally across the middle of Washington State, still healing after ten thousand years. To the south, fir gives way to pine, pine to grass. Cooled basalt lies under ten feet of sandy loam, topped with eight inches of friable dark-brown dust known as loess. Loam and loess, foam and froth, a ghost ocean, undulating in lentil and wheat, remembering waves and beaches from some distant epoch.

The expansive view reminds me of the boy, how he's grown. Earth churns in perpetual motion, the landscape shifts, lifts, and blows away. We live in a stop-motion frame in the earth's story. Our whole life, a transition from one form to another.

The Path of Water

Beginning in early March, snowpack from the mountains around Hayden Lake in Idaho begins to melt, flowing down in streams and creeks to the lake. While much of the lakeshore property has been developed with expensive homes, the Richards, generous easement donors, believed in the importance of protecting land for clean water.

Their land, at the south end of the lake, is the exit point for this cold, clear snowmelt. Here, the water filters through gravels deposited thousands of years ago in the ice age floods and settles in the Spokane Valley Rathdrum Prairie Aquifer.

The aquifer, a massive layer of sand and gravel saturated with water, underlies the broad valley extending from North Idaho to the Spokane metro area. The aquifer provides drinking water to over 600,000 residents in the Inland Northwest and supports thriving ecosystems in this diverse landscape. One of the healthiest in the world, the aquifer is still under threat of increasing drought, pollution, and overdevelopment, making this sensitive aquifer recharge area near Hayden even more important.

Over 90 million gallons of water a day leave Hayden Lake and go into the aquifer. And eight years later, this same cold, clear water bubbles out of the hillside and into the Little Spokane River (a tributary of the Spokane River) at the Conservancy's Waikiki Springs Nature Preserve in North Spokane. This beautiful place is one of the healthiest intact habitats for anadromous fish in the state, primarily because of the addition of cool aquifer water.

Sadly, for more than 100 years, salmon had been banished from these waters. But in August of 2021, in partnership with the Conservancy and Washington Department of Fish and Wildlife, the Spokane Tribe of Indians released 51 adult Chinook salmon into the Little Spokane River at the Conservancy's Waikiki Springs Nature Preserve. These salmon spent the autumn moving upriver, resulting in the spawning of five redds and the stirrings of salmon and clean water advocates throughout the community.

Opposite: Stewards of the land in training gear up for a wetland restoration planting in the Peone Prairie, on the flanks of Mt. Spokane.

Spokane Valley - Rathdrum Prairie Aquifer

Washington

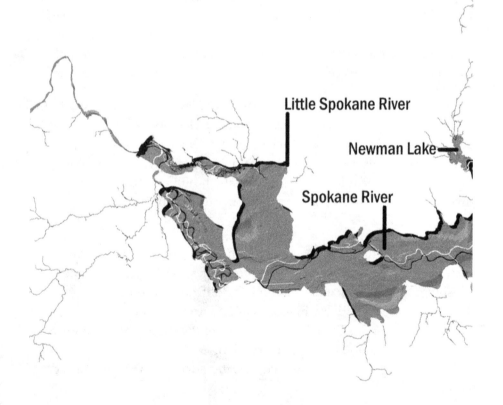

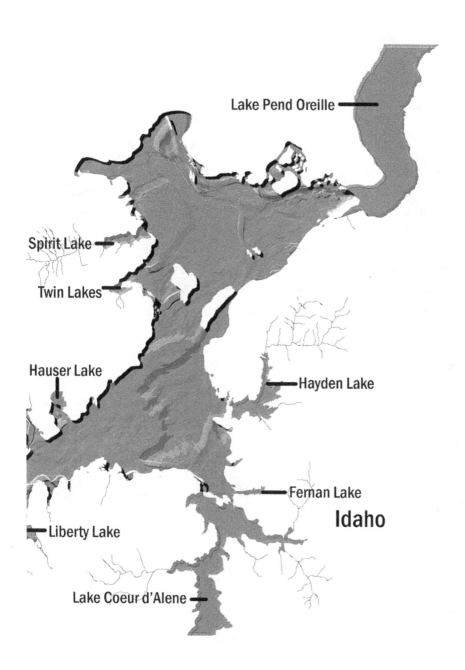

Lake Pend Oreille

Spirit Lake

Twin Lakes

Hauser Lake

Hayden Lake

Fernan Lake

Idaho

Liberty Lake

Lake Coeur d'Alene

Coeur d'Alene River

The Coeur d'Alene river corridor stirs me. Birdwatchers have taken me under their wing and shown me the great marshes and meadows, home to enormous flocks of birds making their ancient way to northern nesting grounds. Recently I learned that tens of thousands of them travel through at night! The Cornell Lab's "Birdcast" uses patterns and radar to predict and count them. Right now, some of my favorites that are passing through nightly are the Swainson's Thrush, Western Tanager, and Spotted Sandpiper by the thousands.

For 20 years I've also explored old homesteads, lands the Conservancy watches over along the river and around the lake. There's magic in an apple from a gnarled, long-abandoned tree. Or a pear. Or old lilac bushes or locust trees, planted centuries ago by the cabin door.

There is a sinister silence too, in the hidden sediments in the floodplains. Sediments laced with a legacy of Silver Valley mining waste, heavy metals like arsenic and lead, flushed into floodplains during spring floods, within reach of the tundra swans feeding with their long necks. But the Conservancy and the Restoration Partnership have found the areas most easily brought back to life so that swans and other creatures can again feed safely and carry on their age-old migrations.

—-Chris DeForest, Inland Northwest Land Conservancy Senior Conservationist

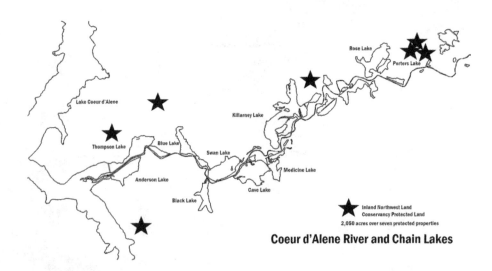

Coeur d'Alene River and Chain Lakes

Sweet Words
—in memory of Neva Hatfield Baker, 1894-1988*
by Kim Barnes

Cross country pen pals romance wary
Old maid train bum two years married
Gunnysack refrigerator spring cold water
Log camp wood sink bear in the cellar
Grizzly Creek windstorm trees roaring down
Tunnel twister bomb blast run honey now
Water in the donkey engine dry to the bone
Piano on the railcar time to call my own
First birth second birth two babes dead
Three more chicken pox not so bad
Bacon in my daughter's throat bacon in my hand
Ten dollar dance fight dreaming big band
Flood stage wall high piano made of mud
Bullet in the neighbor's chest killer red with blood
Long years nursing home five plots gone
River run wind song on my way home

*Words and images from Bert and Marie Russell's interview with Neva Hatfield Baker, November 6, 1974, included in North Fork of the Coeur d'Alene River, Oral History Series, Book No. 3, pp 1-8. Harrison, Idaho: Lacon Publishers, 1984.

Trout Fry in a Shallow
by Robert Wrigley

A universe to the fry, their river.
Fingerlings a month from today.
Translucent, they do not quiver
but shimmer with water going its way
wherever, just as starlight will.

This shank of shallow water's safe
and cooled by a side-current tendril.
They're too small for the osprey's strafe.

But hold out your hand to cast a shadow
and a school will gather in the shape
of your hand, a silver shimmerglow
swimming, a shadow tail, your fingers' cape.

Close to a fist and see them form
a bludgeon at the end of your wrist,
and when you pull back your arm
they dissipate like a living mist.

Coeur d'Alene River Basin Path by Amalia Fisch (Watercolor and Ink on Paper)

☼

Download the free SoundWave Picture app in the Play Store or the Apple App Store and scan this image to hear spring in the Inland Northwest.

Palisades Park

Rimrock to Riverside Healing Balm

The Conservancy's Stewardship Director Rose Richardson shares her recipe for a healing salve, made from foraged ingredients at our Rimrock to Riverside project area, along Spokane's west rim.

Long before we called it Rimrock to Riverside, the Spokane Tribe had a strong presence there. They, the original stewards of that place, cultivated and took care of the native plants that are gathered to make this medicinal salve. Their relationship to these plant species is unique, it is largely thanks to their knowledge that we know about the medicinal values of each of these plants, and many plants exist on the Rimrock to Riverside landscape because of their work and care.

Uses
As an ointment to soothe cuts, burns (including sunburns), or dry cracked skin
As a balm to rub on sore muscles, bruises, or joint pain, For external use only!

Ingredients
½ cup of Infused Oil
Arrowleaf Balsamroot leaves and flowers, *Balsamorhiza sagittate*
Common Yarrow leaves and flowers, *Achillea millefolium*
Common Mullein leaves, *Verbascum thapsus*
Mountain Arnica flowers, *Arnica montana*
Stinging Nettle leaves, *Urtica dioica*
Woods Rose petals, *Rosa woodsii*
Common Dandelion leaves, *Taraxacum officinale*
Optional: English Lavender flowers, *Lavandula angustifolia*
2 Tbsp organic beeswax pastilles
1 Tbsp organic shea butter

Equipment
3-ounce metal salve tin or tinted jar
Cheese cloth
Medium-sized glass jar
Medium-sized pot or saucepan
Stirring stick

Instructions
1. Carefully and sparingly gather the plants and place in a sealable jar. Cover plants in a light oil (vegetable oil, fractionated coconut oil, almond oil, sunflower oil), and allow to sit, sealed, in a warm place, like a sunny windowsill. Shake every few days to get oil moving through the plants.

2. Once your herbs have been steeping for at least a month, strain herbs from the oil using the cheesecloth, pouring the oil into a medium-size, clean jar (the small jar the oil steeped in will be too small).

3. Add the beeswax and shea butter to the oil.

4. Put the jar into a medium-sized pot or saucepan, and fill slightly with water, so the oil level is equal to or below the water level. We're creating a make-shift double-boiler here, folks!

5. Make sure your 3 oz silver salve tin is clean, open, and ready on your counter.

6. Heat the pot over medium-high heat on the stove to start melting the beeswax and shea butter.

7. Watch the beeswax carefully, stirring occasionally with the popsicle stick. As soon as the beeswax is fully melted, remove from heat.

8. Next, pour the (now liquid) salve into the metal tin and set aside to cool and harden. It might take a few hours to harden fully.

NOTE: *Before using, test it by using a small amount on your forearm to make sure you won't have an allergic reaction to any ingredients in the salve. Use at your own risk.*

Rimrock to Riverside
by DJ Lee

for Rose

did the ponds have names? // we'd returned home to find their
sharpness fading // the yellow-headed blackbirds // we heard their
rusty-hinged cries and realized we were happy // service berry, bulrush,
willow // we loosened our grip on life, stopped glancing over our
shoulders every few steps // one day, she told us, she was leaning against
this big ponderosa // we were close to life's borders // the ponds dried
up in winter and resurfaced in spring // we kept reminding ourselves
the day had happened at all // red winged blackbirds, songs like summer
mountains, and starlings mimicking the blackbirds // when we tried to
savor the happiness it dissolved into an aftertaste // aspen, she said, were
the first to come back after the fire // we'd been afraid something would
snatch our lives from us before we reached the end // she'd reached the
point of fully meditating when a thud landed on the earth next to her—
porcupine poop // we wanted to never cross-dissolve back into our
mundane lives // it was rare she came out in spring and didn't see moose,
bobcat, coyote, deer, white tail and mule // to hold life loosely, a ball
bouncing freely on our fingers // the ponds didn't used to dry up, but
they did now // to hold the shutter open indefinitely, one scene blurring
into the next // the birds were erecting leaved nests in the cattails //
to live in the corridor // she pointed to a fire line, to the vanished
ponderosa // so all our days would run together and never stop // she
had no idea he was above her but porcupines can climb // it was to be
expected in this channeled scabland // she saw him, she saw him seeing
her // no, she said, none of the ponds had names—they didn't name
themselves, why should we?

Waikiki Springs Nature Preserve

Strands
by Maiah A Merino

"River, do you remember how it used to be?. . . .For thousands of years, we walked your banks and used your waters. You would always answer when our chiefs called to you with their prayer to the River Spirit. River! Do you remember us?"—-Chief Alex Sherwood, as quoted in Hill, M. "The River Gives us Our Way of Life" in The Spokane River *Ed. Paul Lindholdt, University of Washington Press, Seattle, 2018, p 96*

I came
    —honoring
this place—these people
with a song and tobacco

braiding prayers—
aware
I was taught
braiding is allowed
after you've caught and
released
    what once was

A doorway
between the past
    and present
between us   and Salmon
    honored
111 years remembered

    a future
for the children.
our thoughts
and feelings
pass through us

like the waters who
redeem—
a June Hog Salmon
requiem

we sing
  asking to bring
  understanding
  asking to
  reclaim the land
  we hold hands with
   as we braid

       we braid
         what happens to a place
         when a Spirit returns?
         we learn
         pieces of the
         foundation
         still exist
          persist

   each song
   carries a different
   weight, in its step
   momentum developed

Sanborn
Selheim
Hall
Graves
they came
     remodeled natural relations

   each strand,
    an invitation
    holds
     transferred
      memory
        like family, The River
        invited me
        sitting by the Spring
        —she crawled
        into my lap
        —the red and black ant

matching my
        red and black dress—
yes, together
family, visitors
braiding-unbraiding

between/with children
exploring their worlds—
where Rivers and
Lands connect

reflect
unraveled braids
days we release
the weight and
breathe again

together,
combing through
        our return
            to our
                natal streams.

together,
combing through
wonder and grief
like the pond
once a dumping
        spot for cow feces—
we invite the
songs the
River remembers—

together, combing
the Land—the Salmon
our strands,
long grasses
entangled
        together.

Photo (licensed): Spokane Tribal elder Pat Moses gets a splash as he releases one of 51 Chinook salmon, which appeared in *The Spokesman-Review* **August 6, 2021. Cowles Publishing/** *The Spokesman-Review*

"Sometimes even now I find a lonely spot where the river still runs wild. I find myself talking to it, I might ask, 'River, do you remember how it used to be - the game, the fish, the pure water, the roar of the falls, boats, canoes, fishing platforms? You fed and took care of our people then. For thousands of years we walked your banks and used your waters. You would always answer when our chiefs called to you with their prayer to the river spirit.' Sometimes I stand and shout, 'RIVER, DO YOU REMEMBER US?'"—*Chief Alex Sherwood of the Spokane Tribe, 1973**

---

* as quoted in the Epilogue by Bob Dellwo in Fahey, John. *The Spokane River: Its Miles and Its History.* 1988 (Spokane: WA: The Spokane Centennial Trail Committee). Accessed online: 6/21/22 *http://www. waterplanet.ws/pdf/wpavista20070106.pdf*

KANSAS LAND TRUST

 Kansas

Since 1990, the Kansas Land Trust (KLT) has been working with landowners, communities, and other conservation organizations to protect lands of ecological, agricultural, scenic, historic, and recreational significance in Kansas.

To date, KLT has preserved more than 40,000 acres in Kansas. Within those 40,000 protected acres are more than 30,000 acres of virgin prairie, 173 miles of streambanks, 3,500 acres of prime farmland, and 3,200 acres of woodlands

Our vision for the future of Kansas is one of a flourishing natural heritage that includes:
- Thriving tallgrass prairies filled with native plants that provide wildlife habitat and food for our pollinators.
- Rivers and streams surrounded by robust vegetation that filters runoff and improves the quality of the water running through our faucets.
- Agricultural lands with rich soil where farmers can grow food for our tables.
- Hearty woodlands that can withstand invasive species and provide hiking opportunities in all seasons.

-Wells Farm—Caryn Mirriam-Goldberg
-Priariewood—Traci Brimhall

Wells Farm

Wells Farm is located on the south ridge of the Wakarusa River valley, surrounding Wells Overlook Park, three miles from Lawrence, Kansas. The 130-acre parcel—in the Kansas Land Trust and in the Wells Family since 1866—is a mix of small crop fields, native prairie and woodlands that is dominated by a north-facing osage cuesta, or hill with steep east-west-north slopes and gradual slope to the south.

I've lived here since 1995 with my husband, Ken Lassman, a descendent of William Dougal Wells, who came to the Lawrence area as a member of the third party of the New England Emigrant Society in 1854. Ken has lived on the land almost continuously since 1964 and has managed the land in recent decades for prairie and woodland restoration projects.

A grant from the Douglas County Heritage Council recognizes the unique relationship between the this conservation easement and Wells Overlook Park, a 16-acre park donated to Douglas County by Ken's grandfather, William H. Wells, to honor his family and to share the vista of the surrounding land from atop one of the tallest hills in the county. The county put a large overlook tower on top; in recent years, Ken worked with the county, University of Kansas Dirt Works Studios, Douglas County Historical Society, and Douglas County Master Gardeners to add a wheelchair accessible Passerine Pavilion and Polaris Pavilion to open up the history and views to all people.

I fell in love with this land when I first walked it in 1983, joining Ken in his long-held dream of saving this land from development while also restoring the prairie and woods. With no road map on how to protect this land from development pressures, we met, agonized, prayed, and worked with family, friends and the community for 35 years on how to navigate through an exceedingly difficult family legal trust that made any forward motion almost impossible. On December 15, 2020, we bought the land, and through the considerable efforts of the Kansas Land Trust, this land will be preserved forever.

I wrote these poems from the front screened-in porch of the passive solar home Ken and I designed and built in 1995. I'm deeply grateful to be part of the land, which has shaped and infused my poetry with a sense of homecoming and wonder.

—-Caryn Mirriam-Goldberg
June 2022

Photos: Wells Farm by Jerry Jost

Three Walking Songs for the Night
by Caryn Mirriam-Goldberg

1.
I walk across a field. No more destination,
journey through or over water.
No more dreams of arriving.

I'm here, overlooking a small slope
that leads nowhere. Leaves drop out
of the wet branches. The field eats them.

A fox. Then the sky turns itself
like a clever hand this way and that,
blocking or letting through the moon.

Sometimes rain falls. No matter.
The animals come anyway.
When it clears, I lie on the fallen grass,
look at the brave sky,
and tell myself, "shut up and trust that."

2.
When I wake in the dark, I will go to the forest
with no flashlight, and walk slowly, afraid,
letting my feet make out where next to step,
waiting for what's hidden to let me into its hiding.
No longer dreaming of his hands cupping my head
tenderly, I will just walk in, feeling only
where to land, the noise of the running world no longer running,
the tree frogs cupping their motor song over
the motor song of the cicadas, the brush of branch
on branch, the owls a broken harmonic.

Oh, dream of being loved so perfectly,
Oh, dream of forgiveness,
Oh, damp moon in a pool of clouds,
wide stillness of nothing that we call sky,
now, please let me be brave enough.

3.
I was afraid most of that year.
No particular reason.
Just the rush of old air through my lungs
as if it had nothing better to do.

I'd wake a lot at night, puppy diving
after the kitten, the baby nightmaring
right into the center of my good dream.
I'd wake for nothing also,

sit up, climb out of bed, walking the house
to prove to myself there was no reason
to be afraid. I mean, look at that moon
carrying itself branch to tree branch.
Look at the indentations the wind makes
of its body in the grass.

See how round the earth is,
remember how many animals sleep
hidden like prayers in the tall grass.

See the open mouth of the sky, the shifting of stars
across the throat of the universe,
this time in its slot actually happening.

☼

Burning the Prairie
by Caryn Mirriam-Goldberg

1.
A field is a black hole, shadow made solid
fastened to the ground.
The skull of a baby deer lies there
in the old black hair.
The closed entrance to a mouse house
in dirt that filters sunlight
like the heart filters blood.
I stand on the field's ledge, think about the past,
charred only where I've touched it.
The stories of one slow burn or another.
How much water is there in the world anyway?

Not enough, says the inside of a cave.
Not enough, says the snippet of lilac in the bedroom.
Not enough, says this field.

2.
Years ago, my husband was burning a field
when the field started burning him back.
Caught in the change of wind
clanging the flames closer so they could do
what they long to do most their whole fire life
– rush up a huge sheet of brilliance –
he did the only thing to save his life:
he ran through the fire.

3.
A duck cries. I dream I'm standing
in the burned field again, but before it was burned.
I don't like all this tangle and height.
I want the future cleared away,
absent and present at once.

4.
We burn the field so the grass
can have its house back,
clean out the houseguest-from-hell trees,
sweep the floors, open the windows
to let the smoke out.

We burn the field so that we, ignorant to the black sky,
can see sheet after wavy sheet of burning,
and call it beauty.

We burn the field to start something we can't stop
and then stop it.

5.
After the burn, I hold my husband's hand
in the bedroom like it's a candle
I wouldn't want to tip toward
all that dry, all that's above ground.

No one talking, the dark as heavy
inside as it is out, the ceiling fan swooshing
us still. I am scared to lie here with the wind
so high, the tangle and brush of us ready.

How easy to start a fire.
How untrue that ripeness comes only
to the wet and lush.

Coordinates
by Caryn Mirriam-Goldberg

I live just south of the poetic,
where the glaciers stopped short, sloped down
to nothing. Now low-flying catfish line
the brown rivers while the valleys go flat
as clavicles edging into erosion and horizon.
The grass, obsessive as always,
runs itself oblivious,
and the cedar trees wave,
one arm, then another,
as if under water.

I live where the sky, dense and
exhausted, complains all smug and blue
that nothing ever happens here,
and leans asleep on its elbows in the corner.
It dreams what we mean: that we can only
locate ourselves in the weather that maps us
but can't be mapped ahead of itself.

Here there's no way to know what's coming,
or what's gone, the big bluestem as tall as it is.
The wind comes. The wind goes. The sun climbs
around the corner and returns at its appointed time.
The windows shake in the storm that can pick up
a field, undress it, place it back down.

When I try to say where I am, I can only
point to the rushing everywhere
the mind tries to be still,
and in that wind, the stillness
that holds a single glance of switchgrass
up to the light before letting it go.

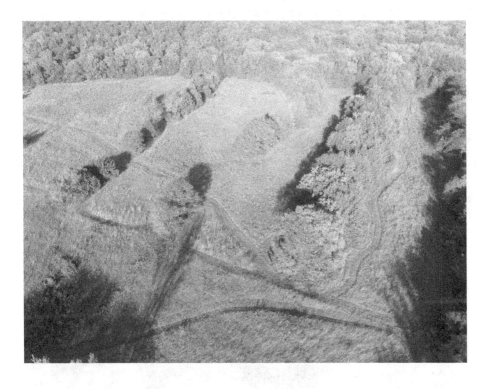

Photo: Wells Farm by Jerry Jost

Prairiewood

*Prairiewood is part of 500 acres of preserved tallgrass prairie in the Flint Hills.
This area was once part of a vast inland sea, but like all places, its story has changed
with time. The Kaw, Osage, and Pawnee once managed these lands, and now it is some
of the last tallgrass prairie in the world. I felt so lucky to get to walk these trails and
to have such strikingly different encounters each time I did. Each time I went out, my
only goal was to be present, to notice the things I saw and heard and felt. Of course, I
also brought my other thoughts with me and found myself writing about more than the
flora and fauna of the place. In the end it helped me see how interconnected all living
things are, even when I believe my griefs and joys are separate from the world around
me.*

—-Traci Brimhall
May 2022

Photo: Prairiewood by Ryan Kegley

Prairie Ecology
by Traci Brimhall

First, the side oats grama playing companion
to wildflowers, and then blue sage lodging

on goldenrod as if the whole prairie urged me
to depend on you. Though the pink flash

of grasshopper wings makes me think *solitude*
and a prickly pear in the path guards itself alone,

the kaleidoscope of butterflies puddling on
cow pies gives me pause. The day began with

a single wild turkey so startled it flew from me,
but then a committee of vultures in the trees rose

to become a kettle. Anything can become a sign
if I let it, but I am trying to listen with care,

to trust last year's hedge apples that seem to say
abundance. By the pond you say, *Listen*—and I do,

as spring peepers plop into deeper water's safety.
I admire the raw orange of a lone exposed root

in the mud, and we hear the nicker of warning.
Three horses appear sudden as evening shadows

behind us, hooves tamping damp earth. We are
nothing to them. Their teeth tug at the fresh grass,

ears flexed in our direction but content. Like me,
they trust themselves to know if they need to run.

Though they are beautiful, we're afraid of our
smallness. My body says *Be careful,* but the tickle

I feel is only you reaching for me so we can both
take custody of this memory–how love is an ecology

of awe that takes turns growing and feasting, a simple
sublime and with you, finally, breathless and blooming.

Photo: Prairiewood by Jerry Jost

Devotional
by Traci Brimhall

I come looking for many of the miracles I find—
the first yellow of April, a redbud pinking with spring,
lichen silvering the conifer branches. Other graces

find me too—the wind carving its way along the ridge,
stumps of trees licked black by lightning, even the music
of light hail on last year's leaves and the hymn of acorn

cupules crunching underfoot. Even before blackbird nests
clutch eggs or bison calve, everything radiates with life.
Golden flowers hallelujah at the road's edge. A lone tree

bends like a penitent over the pond. Even if I wanted to
inch out on its trunk to dip my hand in the water, none
of this beauty wants me to love it too closely. No gentle

stroke of feather or hide, even branches shaking with
squirrels raise their new green tips too high to reach.
Everything wants the intimacy of beholding, which is

an intimacy that requires distance. Only deer tracks
in the sand let me slip a finger in the print of each mark,
only empty pods of wild indigo let me grab and rattle.

The living only welcome me if I hold myself as quiet
as a prayer, still as a heron, let the seeds be touched
awake by rain tithing itself to the dirty heaven at my feet.

Anniversary
by Traci Brimhall

This year, cloud shadows glide
like a funeral procession across
emerald grasses. Ground plums
swell, the sun rounds higher,
and unsentimental flies clean
what the hawk left by the trail.
Across hills stitched with limestone,
a dusty cluster of grazing bison.
From here they look as tiny as
hummingbird eggs, like I could
lose them in the creases of my palm
if I tried to hold them. Another year
and still I remember how to count
the approaching storm's miles, to carry
twice the water I need, that breadroot
can feed me, that bitter yarrow can
heal me. I still struggle to love
this world without you.

Photo Above: Prairiewood by Jerry Jost
Photo Below: Wells Farm by Jerry Jost

Photo: Prairiewood by Jerry Jost

THE NATURE CONSERVANCY

Kansas

The Nature Conservancy works to create a world where people and nature thrive. Our mission is to conserve the lands and waters on which all life depends. In the Flint Hills of Kansas, we're protecting the world's last significant expanse of tallgrass prairie, working with ranchers to implement conservation stewardship, and preventing it from conversion.

Once sprawling from central Canada to the Gulf of Mexico, the tallgrass prairie has been plowed under, developed, or overrun with invasive plants and trees. Less than 4% remains, most of which is found in eastern Kansas and northern Oklahoma. Here remains nearly four million acres of deep-rooted grasses that nurture some of the greatest biological diversity in the world.

The Nature Conservancy safeguards 120,000 acres of tallgrass prairie in the Flint Hills. Approximately half of that is at nature preserves owned by The Nature Conservancy Tallgrass Prairie National Preserve (in Chase County, Kansas) and the Joseph H. Williams Tallgrass Prairie Preserve (in Osage County, Oklahoma) welcome visitors to explore the prairie by hiking, birdwatching, and viewing the bison herds. The other half is protected through conservation easements on privately-owned land. These voluntary but permanent easements strategically connect our nature preserves to create passageways for wildlife throughout the landscape. Learn more at nature.org/flinthills

-Flint Hills—Denise Low

Flint Hills

Jackrabbit
by Denise Low

The Flint Hills stretch to infinity—an abstract word meeting
you here on this hill. The motion in grass

might be wind but no, the jagged path shows where a bony
jackrabbit flees. They fear people.

This autumn afternoon disappears as sun rouges the west or maybe
it continues in another dimension.

Listen. Your breath ripples the bluestem grass. Your eyes see
beyond the creek leading sky to darkness.

Past and future merge at the horizon and last forever. You travel
this kingdom with Coronado, before he left

Quivera, before he wrote about land "so vast I did not find
the limit anywhere I went."

Some days thunderheads explode in the skies with lightning bolts
so loud the ground shakes. Rainbows follow.

Millions of stars speckle the night. All people who once lived here
surround us. Red-tail hawks keep watch.

Photo: Jackrabbit © Frank Klein/TNC Photo Contest 2019

Photo: Flint Hills Sunset © Jim Griggs-Selective Focus

Flint Hills Grass Ocean
by Denise Low

Grass hovers above earth   grazes sky
multiple strands of warp dangling.   No weft

but a line of vole nests along   horizons
at your feet. Sky begins at   ground-level.

No illusion   Rocky Mountain gusts
lost for miles stop at your back   push

a hard hand   between shoulder blades.
Wind probes   your flesh-covered wings.

Lift feet.   You fly with seed heads
ever eastward   the downstream pattern

traced in air like stems flattened   the same
direction after a flood.   Dragonflies circle ponds.

Open your fingers.   Like grass, you feel
forces beyond your control.   You feel belief.

Council Grove Reservoir: American Vultures
by Denise Low

Black angels—buzzards—
roost every other post

along the pier. This powder blue
afternoon juggles a lemon sun.

Below, a trapped river muddles
the lake's surface. Underwater

spirits call to each other
in currents, repeating names:

Wildcat Creek, Canning Creek,
Short Creek, the Neosho.

Wind sweeps away traces
of all tongues. Vanished

are buffalo hunters, drovers,
women and swaddled babies—

all who passed through these hills
on the journey to Paradise.

Flint
by Denise Low

Bear-brown stones of my hometown
turn up in arrowhead collections
miles away chipped into points
of interest. Also blades and tips.

I saw one embedded in a skull
on a girl scout trip to the museum
before stolen bones were reburied.
A solid stuck in another solid.

A Ho-Chunk man Darren Snake
drove with us through the hills
amazed at miles of flint. Easy
to stop and fill a bag full.

Not dull dirt but its coppery sheen—
beauty of pressed quartz—shines,
fractured along lay lines of power
and weakness. Sharp when broken.

Hefty palm-sized nodules fit
into the hand. Fingers closed,
the ax is ready, fight ready.
Or flint lies face down. Waits.

Defining the Flint Hills
by Brian Obermeyer and Rex Buchanan*

Photo: Exposed rocks at Konza Biological Research Station, a Nature Conservancy preserve in the Flint Hills that is managed by Kansas State University's division of biology as a field research station © Mark Godfrey/TNC

The Flint Hills may be the best-loved natural area in Kansas. As the largest intact tallgrass prairie remaining in all of North America, it is also the state's most ecologically significant landscape. The Flint Hills stretch north to south across east-central Kansas and even extend on down into Oklahoma (where they are called the Osage Hills). The region's width is relatively uniform, averaging perhaps 50 miles but reaching 75 miles at the widest.

But how, exactly, do you define the Flint Hills? And precisely where do they start and stop?

These might seem like simple questions, but they're not, really. The answers depend on the characteristics you take into account.

* Rex Buchanan and Brian Obermeyer, 2012 *Symphony in the Flint Hills Field Journal*, Volume IV. Reprinted with permission.

If asked to define the Flint Hills, some might say it is a region of bluestem grass (tallgrass prairie) where layers of limestone have been sculpted by erosion. Others might assume that, by definition, the Flint Hills are a hilly region of pastureland where flint (also known as chert) is scattered about. Flint is embedded within limestone layers in the Flint Hills; both flint and limestone are sedimentary rocks. Because flint, consisting of silicon dioxide, is much harder than the surrounding limestone, it often survives erosion and can be found littering the ground's surface.

Lieutenant Zebulon Pike, who led an expedition across the Flint Hills in 1806, painfully discovered this fact. Pike remarked in his journal, "Passed very ruff [sic] flint hills. My feet blistered and very sore." The underlying chert and limestone were neither appreciated by Pike nor his feet, but it is the principal reason the Flint Hills are still in native prairie. An Osage Indian reportedly once told a homesteader with a plow strapped to his wagon, "you won't put that iron thing here." While the homesteader may not have appreciated the quip, the land's resistance to plowing turned out to be a blessing in disguise, ensuring that a landscape expression of tallgrass prairie would survive. Today, roughly two-thirds of what remains of the historic tallgrass prairie is found in the Flint Hills.

> **Only about 4% of the original tallgrass prairie remains. Roughly two-thirds of what does remain is found in the Flint Hills of Kansas and Oklahoma.**

While thin, chert-strewn soils characterize a sizable area of the Flint Hills, not every layer of Flint Hills limestone contains flint. And along the eastern flank of the Flint Hills, for example, one encounters a landscape that looks very much like the Flint Hills, but the rock layers that commonly contain flint are absent. So it may not be useful to define the Flint Hills according to the presence, or absence, of flint.

Geologists sometimes define regions according to the age of the rocks found there. In the case of the Flint Hills, all of the bedrock (the layers of limestone, shale, and other consolidated rocks that are common here) is Permian in age, deposited about 300 million years ago. The rocks just to the east are slightly older, deposited in the Pennsylvanian period of geologic history, and the rocks to the west are generally younger.

While it might be possible, at least geologically, to define the Flint Hills as an area of native prairie with rocks of Permian age, that definition would include some areas, particularly the west side of the Hills, where the landscape is lacking rolling topography and flint-bearing limestones that are typically associated with the Flint Hills. What's more, some hilly areas of Pennsylvanian age east of the Flint Hills are virtually indistinguishable from the Flint Hills, such as the remnant prairies of Anderson County.

Photo: Showy Evening Primrose at Tallgrass Prairie National Preserve © Chris Helzer

Another geologic similarity across much of the Flint Hills is the lack of glaciation; most of the Flint Hills landscape lies south of the farthest advance of glaciers. But in the extreme northeastern portion, including northern Wabaunsee County, one can still see rocks called erratics that were left behind about 400,000 years ago when a glacier moved into northeastern Kansas. The most common is Sioux Quartzite, a pink metamorphosed sandstone that dates back a billion years; occasionally, other glacial hitchhikers are found, such as granite and agate.

These examples show that as important as geology is, it is not the only factor in defining the Flint Hills. A more modern approach to define and delineate a landscape like the Flint Hills is through shared climate and geology, a method typically used to define ecoregions; this approach assumes that geology and climate largely determine the distribution of plants and animals.

> # More than 600 different species of plants are found in tallgrass prairie.

The Nature Conservancy uses a slightly broader definition that considers not only commonalities of geology, climate, and even land use, but also ecological attributes (e.g., landscape ecological functional size and the distribution of flora and fauna). This approach describes the Flint Hills (or Greater Flint Hills) as a landform where intact, tallgrass prairie is the dominant vegetation type (as identified via interpretations of satellite imagery). More specifically, the Greater Flint Hills is a contiguous landscape of tallgrass prairie with species characteristic of the Flint Hills eco-region.

This broader definition also characterizes the Flint Hills as a landscape sculpted by erosion with gently sloping hills, with an elevational relief of 300 to 500 feet in the more eroded areas. Climate is influenced by the landscape's position within the interior of the continent. Hot continental summer temperatures and cool winters (with occasional arctic blasts) are the norm. The Rocky Mountain rain shadow to the west is tempered by occasional moisture-laden airflow from the Gulf of Mexico. Annual precipitation varies from about 25 to 35 inches. Deeper soils adjacent to stream courses allow cultivation of crops, whereas ranching is the principal land use in the uplands. Cattle grazing and the frequent burning of prairies are common and accepted practices. And, of course, many of the outcroppings of rocks are limestone, cherty limestones, and shale. Because it can grow so tall, big bluestem is the grass most people identify with tallgrass prairie, but little bluestem, Indiangrass, sideoats grama, and switchgrass are also common, along with the many lesser-known grasses (nearly 90 species in all) and an ever-changing panorama of flowering plants (wildflowers). In the early spring, there's the showy yet delicate yellow to orangish flowers of Missouri evening primrose, petite pink to purple flowers of ground-plum milk-vetch, and lavender petals of spiderwort, to name just a few. The prairie really comes alive in early summer, with such species and colors as butterfly milkweed (yellow to deep orange), lead plant (blue to violet), wild alfalfa or scurfy pea (light blue to purple), compass plant (yellow), and blue wild indigo (purplish blue). In autumn, light blue blossoms of pitcher sage and bright yellow Maximilian's sunflower stand out against the dormant reddish-gold grasses.

So, with this new, broad definition in mind, where you enter the Flint Hills will determine what you see.

Photo: Tallgrass Prairie National Preserve Hills © Tom Gross

Photo: Angus Ranchers on Horseback © Ryan Donnell

If you come from the east on U.S. Highway 56, you entered the Flint Hills just north of the town of Admire, a few miles west of the intersection between the Kansas Turnpike and U.S. 56. The landscape takes on a rolling aspect, and the rocks are Permian in age. The predominant land use is cattle grazing on tallgrass prairie; relatively little ground is cultivated here. Even though that's about where the Flint Hills start, you won't encounter your first flint-bearing limestone until you were about ten miles west of Admire, where U.S. 56 cuts through a rock layer called the Threemile limestone, which is loaded with chert. In fact, the hills west of Bushong include layers of this cherty Threemile limestone.

Coming in on U.S. 56 from the west, you'll first encounter the Flint Hills around the town of Marion, where the county courthouse is built out of Cottonwood limestone, a thick, blocky limestone that is identified strongly with the Flint Hills (even though it contains relatively little chert).

Coming up the Kansas Turnpike from Wichita, the Turnpike runs through Permian rocks around Wichita, but this flat landscape is very different from the Flint Hills, which you would first encounter about ten miles east of the Sedgwick County/Butler County line, where the landscape again takes on the rolling aspect that characterizes the Flint Hills. This is also about where you would see the Winfield Limestone (named for the town of Winfield), which includes layers of chert.

Obviously, you could enter and experience the Flint Hills in other ways, just as there are different ways to define the Flint Hills. Because definitions are subjective and maps will likely be refined by future mapmakers, maybe a "know-it-when-you-see-it" approach is the best way to confirm your arrival.

But, here are a few indicators that might help. You might be in the Flint Hills where there are miles upon miles of intact, native tallgrass prairie carpeting smooth-sculpted, rolling hills; where a wind-swept, prairie ridge comes alive each spring morning with the mating calls and dances of greater prairie-chickens; where an orange horizon and the smell of prairie smoke does not cause panic, but is rather a sign that winter has waned; where slabs of limestone form a rim along pasture hillsides; where you can still watch real cowboys moving cattle on horseback; and where an Osage orange (hedge) post is the tallest perch around for an upland sandpiper to perch, raise its wings, and exhale its distinctive "wolf-whistle."

You might be in the Flint Hills where there are miles upon miles of intact, native tallgrass prairie carpeting smooth-sculpted, rolling hills; where a wind-swept, prairie ridge comes alive each spring morning with the mating calls and dances of greater prairie-chickens; where an orange horizon and the smell of prairie smoke does not cause panic, but is rather a sign that winter has waned; where slabs of limestone form a rim along pasture hillsides; where you can still watch real cowboys moving cattle on horseback; and where an Osage orange (hedge) post is the tallest perch around for an upland sandpiper to perch, raise its wings, and exhale its distinctive "wolf-whistle."

Photo (opposite): Monarchs © Richard Hamilton Smith

Photo: Common Milkweed © Chris Helzer

VERMONT LAND TRUST

Vermont Land Trust

Vermont

UNITING LAND AND LIVES

Vermont is a place where the wellbeing of land and people are entwined. This legacy of interdependence is more essential today than ever, as we strive to build a more sustainable and just future. Every day, we work to strengthen and celebrate Vermont's land, its peoples' resourcefulness, and strong sense of community. We champion working farms and forests, support rural communities and their economies, and protect land, water, and soil. We foster healthy connections between land and lives—connections that can take root in a single moment and grow for a lifetime.

Learn more and get involved at vlt.org

- East Montpelier Trails—Jesse LoVasco
- Knoll Farm—Ann B. Day
- Charlotte Park and Wildlife Refuge—Dan Close

East Montpelier Trails

Many communities wish to preserve their unique character. East
Montpelier is one town that has had incredible success doing so. In the
1980s, community members gathered to discuss what their town would
look like in the future. The overwhelming response was to keep the
farms and create a town-wide trail system; a town fund was established to
support this vision and a non-profit organization, East Montpelier Trails
Inc. was formed manage the trails. Over the years, more than 24 parcels
of farm and forestland were conserved with the Vermont Land Trust.
The trail system crosses nearly all of these properties and is maintained
by many dedicated volunteers.

Photo: East Montpelier Trails by VLT

Morning Fog in the Forest
by Jesse LoVasco

Life in the woodland
holds a thousand tongues:
an ecotone of wildflowers,
Purple Asters,
Goldenrod,
Jewelweed.

Spider webs shaped like
hammocks, coated in dew.

Steadfast trees,
upended roots growing
an ecosystem of moss
and lichen evolving.

Always something
letting go in order
to begin again.

Today not one stranger,
not even a birdsong,
but cricket's
suspended call
hovering in morning fog
like a mantra.

Listening Holds the Forest
by Jesse LoVasco

Listening   holds a forest

    like a sacred vessel.

Allowing it to fill

        with voices.

Hermit thrush,   red squirrels

    rustling in detritus of leaves,

drumming wings of grouse,

    owl   in a canopy.

Words muffle the music,

    laughter competes.

        Quiet

reveals the signature of wood songs.

Not held in two hands,

    but with attention

cupped around   wonder.

What Steps To Take
by Jesse LoVasco

My steps are not the bear's,
lumbering through forest ferns
pressing their weight,
clawing bark, reaching berries,

nor are they, thin prints of fox,
arrow to the wind, swiftly scouting
land for mice and moving food.

I am not like wolf, masking my
hunt around stands of trees
and brush, waiting for prey.

Who am I, daring to travel in
this moss covered land, that my
kind have separated from,
without asking questions.

I know nothing.

How do I walk so as not to disturb,
listen so that I do not disrupt,
sit quietly so that all creatures

and plants around me,
are free to fly and run, sense
that my presence is not a threat.

That I will not squash
partridge berry under my feet,
take a birch to the ground,
leave burning coals from
a warming fire.

And like any home that I

enter, not dismantle the
woodland altars that have
spirited the caves and
spaces with their grace.

**Photo: East Montpelier Trails near Cherry Tree Hill
by Jill Sudhoff-Guerin**

Knoll Farm

Ann and Frank Day bought Knoll Farm in 1957, where they raised
Scotch Highland Cattle and welcomed guests from all over the world.
The farm as served as a peace and justice center, and has welcomed
people working for the well-being of humans and the land. Knoll Farm's
purpose has always been relationships: fostering kinship between humans
and nature, understanding and reconciling betrayals between people, and
building our collective ability to meaningfully respond to the crises of
our times. In 1983, Ann Day donated a conservation easement to the
Vermont Land Trust, to ensure the farm's scenic fields, thriving forest
and historic barn would always be protected. Today, Knoll Farm brings
organic food, connection and meaning to communities far and wide.

The Sometimes Brook
by Ann B. Day

On our farm there's
a sometimes brook
that's only there
when you look
at certain times of the year.

Lost beneath ice and snow,
it then is freed and
like a circus tumbler
is watery laughter
we're glad to hear.

It winds the field
with a silvery thread,
then is lost in autumn's shed,
a stillness in the leafy nook.

At last November's
snow and rain brings
again the sweet refrain
of our erratic sometimes brook.

Rhythm of the Forest
by Ann B. Day

We walk the old logging road,
high along the forest's eastern
slope, where spring's morning
sunlight beams through bare
branches of the hardwoods:
maple, oak, beech, butternut
still tight budded in early May.

The forest floor warms under
last year's old leaves as we see
violets, spring beauties, trout lilies
Dutchmen's breeches bloom along
the edges of the road.

By June these flowers will have
begun to fade, fruits and seeds
are forming in their place to
provide seeds and plant food
for birds and mice to eat.

Again, we walk the old road under
unfurling leaves of the hardwoods,
while, deep in the earth, the spring
plants get nourishment from roots
to grow again in next April's sun:

These are the ephemeral plants,
living in rhythm with the trees.
We pause to breathe in the miracle
of newness from the old.

Photo (opposite): Knoll Farm by Ann B. Day

Barn Fantasy
by Ann B. Day

Do not despair
of fast and modern ways
with octane cars and jetting
airplanes.

Instead, repair
up to a hillside barn
that stands against the snow
and summer rains.

A buggy there
invites your rest
upon its seat, away from
stress and strains.

The old bay mare
is gone. But fantasy
returns the slower pace
of wooded lanes.

Birthing on the Farm
by Ann B. Day

It starts in February
with great horned owlets in tree hollows,
black bear sow suckling her cubs in a rocky den,
crusty drifts beginning to melt and spread across

April's brown pastures with ribbons of green,
creating rivulets that flow into brooks and tumble
to the Mad River in the Valley below.

Purple violets, spring beauties, bell worts,
Dutchman's britches, appear along the logging
road on the farm's south facing forest slopes.

Barn swallows return to start mud nests under
shed eaves and bluettes bloom in sun filled fields.
Under a hemlock in the woods above the farm

a doe lies waiting for the birth of her fawn.
Then the *pent, pent* of a woodcock's spiral
flight as he climbs high above a pasture seep.

Now, from the barnyard in today's dawning,
I hear bleating of ewes and their newborn lambs,
the resurrection of life truly has come.

**Photo (opposite): Helen Whybrow feeds the lambs at Knoll Farm
by Ann B. Day**

Charlotte Park and Wildlife Refuge

The Charlotte Park and Wildlife Refuge is a peaceful haven for people and animals. Most of the land was donated to the Town of Charlotte in 1999. The town cares for the land as a park and wildlife refuge. A large portion of the property had been conserved with the Vermont Land Trust in 1998. Trails wind through farmland and meadows, and diverse woodlands and wetlands. Visitors can walk through clayplain forest, a forest type once common in the area, but now rare. The wetlands and grasslands offer excellent birdwatching. And a giant old oak tree is one of the three largest in town.

Critters of the Charlotte Refuge
by Dan Close

Can There Be Panthers About?

Within the realm of predatory beasts, from weasel up to eagle
We have here represented all of them, from bear and fox to beagle
But there is one we cannot count, for there have been no sightings,
The mighty catamount is out, and counted just in mightings.

The Coyote

The coyote who barks in the night
Can throw the whole house in a fright
For his yips are received
By his buddies, indeed –
His posse is poised for the fight.

The Bear

Be aware of the neighborhood bear
He seems to be everywhere
He needs space to roam
Besides at our home
So give him his space, or Beware!

Sailing Moon

The night the moon went sailing across the azure sky
Ah! Well do I remember the pumpkin in its eye.
T'was the brightest moon forever that was seen by you or I,
The night the moon went sailing across the azure sky.

Bees

The bees are on their knees, they say,
But their hives are full of honey.
They toil and buzz throughout the days –
That's how they make their money.
They're just like us in many ways,
They store up all they make, sir,
But when the winter's said and done
They're out again – see how they run
About the surface of their hives.
Their buzzing wings say 'Strive!' 'Survive!'
But still the toxins do attack
And strive bees might, but they do lack
The armaments to fend the toxins off.
We must protect them at all costs
And strive ourselves, come with our aid,
Or we, too, humans, dig our grave.

**Photo: Boardwalk at Charlotte Park and Wildlife Refuge
by Maya Sutton-Smith**

The Beaver
by Dan Close

The beaver, you know, he runs the whole show,
Like any good carpenter does,
First his logs he retrieves, from the bank and the leas,
And smacks them together with mud.
And his pond he then fills, and it fills with bluegills,
Or, with any luck, some kind of trout.
And his home he then builds, with all kinds of frills,
(not the least is the hidden way out)
And his larder he fills, with the branches he mills
And delectable watercress sprouts.

Then the pond it fills up with all kinds of stuff,
Salamanders, amphibians, and such
Who feed on the larvae of mayflies
And other incredible bugs.
And whirligigs whirl and hellgrammites curl
And the nymphs and the naiads do flourish
Then burst through the surface into summer's air
Where they're suddenly seen as if in a dream
To become ancient damsels and dragons,
And they fly through the air and zoom everywhere
In an absolute frenzy of tag-ons.

Well, while all this is happening, the deer comes to drink,
Along with the bear who stands on the brink
And the coyote comes, too, along with the shrew,
And the turtle suns on her log
And eyes the fox who is licking his chops
And wondering what mischief he can do.
While high up above, the eagle she soars,
And the swallows, while flying much lower,
Collect their dinners of surfacing swimmers
Intent on a season of glory, or more.

Meanwhile Missus Beaver is carrying pups

And showing them just how to gnaw their way up
To adulthood, and then they depart
To start their own pond just upriver
From the folks back at home, and with sleek coats do roam
In search of their own pond and dinner.

And so, dear reader, you see the importance
Of beavers in our ecology.
If it weren't for beavers, there would be no spring
For so many species, and what would become of biology?

**Photo: Shady Bench, Charlotte Park and Wildlife Refuge
by Maya Sutton-Smith**

HILLTOWN LAND TRUST

Massachusetts

Hilltown Land Trust works to conserve ecologically important wildlands, economically and culturally important working lands, and the scenic beauty and rural character of the Hilltowns. Our service area includes 13 rural towns in the foothills of the Berkshires in western Massachusetts. Since our founding in 1986, we have protected and continue to steward over 5,000 acres of land.

—Conwell Property

Poet: JuPong Lin

Artwork: Sarah Welch
Photos: Hilltown Land Trust

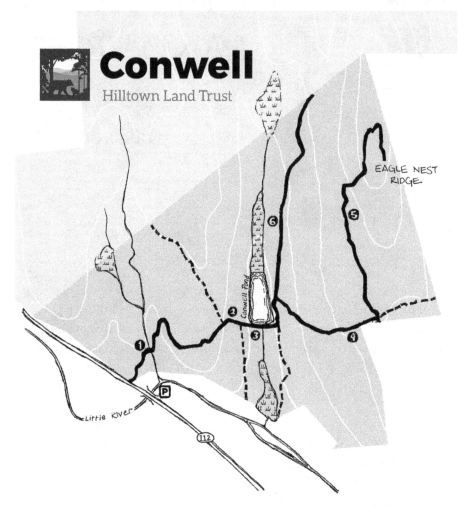

Conwell
Hilltown Land Trust

EAGLE NEST RIDGE

Conwell Pond

Little River

112

Legend

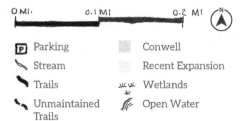

0 MI.   0.1 MI   0.2 MI   N

P Parking
~ Stream
~ Trails
~ Unmaintained Trails

Conwell
Recent Expansion
Wetlands
Open Water

Esoteric Guide

1 Mossy stream crossing
2 Big old white pine
3 Nice place to sit on the dam
4 Split-in-half tree
5 Rock tripe
6 Puffball mushrooms

Conwell Property

An empty wooden stool perches on the edge of a quiet pond at Conwell, beckoning hikers to make the journey in from the trailhead to watch the still waters reflect the shifting colors of the trees ringing its shores.

Photo: A Place to Sit by Conwell Pond

The Conwell Property, 175 acres of forest land featuring 3 miles of Hilltown Land Trust's newest public hiking trails on unceded Nipmuc, Pocumtuc, Woronoco, and Mohican land, is a place of subtle pleasures. Visitors can pause on a warm fall day to see puffball mushrooms blooming flower-like from a rotting log, or climb steadily to the top of Eagle Nest Ridge along the base of lichen-studded cliff faces. On the way back to the trailhead, you might pause at the stream to listen to the water burble gently before crossing with careful balance on moss-covered rocks. Atop the last ridge before reaching the road again, tall pines and red oaks reach skyward, parting briefly to let beams of sun fall to the forest floor.

Photo: A hemlock-lined trail along Conwell Pond

As a land trust, many of our most visible forms of care for the land look like removing fallen logs from trails, posting signage, or blazing a clear path through the woods. Poetry provides a different entry point to a relationship with the land. Walking at Conwell, JuPong has turned her tender attention to tiny red mushrooms, the song of a Carolina wren threaded through rustling oak leaves, and the legacy of Mahican doctor Rhoda Rhodes. Noticing and listening to the land and its stories is its own deep form of care.

Map: Google Earth. Data SIO, NOAA, U.S. Navy, NGA, GEBCO. Image Landsat/Copernicus. Image U.S. Geological Survey

A Five-Toed Path to Conservation

Drawing: American Mink

In 2012 , a wildlife tracking study completed by The Nature Conservancy revealed that American mink (*Neovison vison*) were using the area. This member of the weasel family prefers wetland and stream habitat abundant at Conwell, and the property provided a crucial link for mink to travel between large conservation areas.

When The Nature Conservancy shared how important Conwell was for local mink, landowners Cynthia and Peter Cook were inspired to protect this wildlife corridor. In 2017, they donated 70 acres of the original Conwell property to Hilltown Land Trust.

With support from MassWildlife, Hilltown Land Trust recently added 105 acres to the original 70-acre property connecting Eagle Nest Ridge with the edge of remote Jackson Swamp to the north.

For key species like mink and red fox, as well as all beings who inhabit the area, this newly conserved corridor is a key piece linking thousands of acres of the most important wildlife habitat in Massachusetts. In addition, hikers will soon be able to walk a complete loop over Eagle Nest Ridge, up to Jackson Swamp, and back past Conwell Pond.

"This place packs many features into a small geography – pond, wetland, forest, ridgetop – all of which will be accessible to the public now that the land is conserved," says Hilltown Land Trust Executive Director Sally Loomis. "In addition, there is now a permanent north-south corridor of undeveloped land that is so important to wildlife in the face of climate change."

Photo: Mink build dens in the banks of the Little River, which runs along the southeast edge of Conwell

Parcel boundaries on a map tell one story, one of ownership. What the mink see is another story: clean water; plenty of small rodents and frogs to eat; and safe places to build dens and raise their young. Land conservation looks very different from the perspective of mink, who ask us as stewards to consider the many needs and stories of all life in this place. Because wildlife trackers noticed and listened to the mink, we can continue to care for their habitat for years to come.

Poetry is a mirror that reflects the land's care back on us. Visit Conwell and walk down to the Little River from the parking lot to witness it for yourself. Listen to the music of care in the bright water cascading over rocks, in the fathomless mycelial webs underfoot, and in the five-toed mink tracks on the sandy banks.

Drawing: Mink Tracks

Bridging Wildlife Habitat

▨ HLT-Conserved Land	⁺⁺ NHESP BioMap Core Habitat
▨ Other Conserved Land	▨ NHESP Critical Natural Landscape

0   0.125   0.25   0.5 miles   (N)

American Mink: https://commons.wikimedia.org/wiki/File:American_mink.jpg

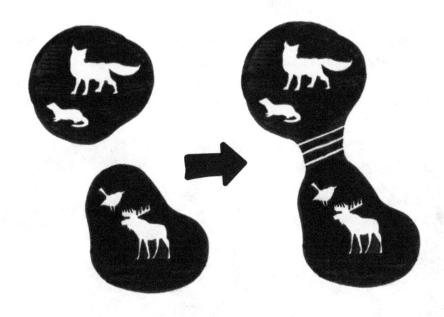

Diagram: Bridging Wildlife Habitat
Drawing: Red Fox

Volunteer Celebration

Volunteers were essential in opening the Conwell property to the public, from helping cut and blaze trails to installing signs and a kiosk. In March of 2022, volunteers, staff, and TerraCorps members gathered to celebrate volunteers' many contributions to Conwell and land conservation all over the Hilltowns.

Photo: Volunteers gather at Conwell to celebrate their contributions to conservation

The group walked together to the edge of Conwell Pond, gathering in a circle to listen to JuPong Lin speak. She described her qigong practice of daily connection to the soil, inviting us to remove our shoes and touch the earth with our feet. Over the soft sound of early-spring snowfall, JuPong read her poem "A Hilltown Pond."

Photo: JuPong Lin reads her poetry

This Hilltown Pond
by JuPong Lin

In the shade of fungus festooned
   hemlock and pine
foxfire blued twigs and tender
   trickling of a stream
melting mysteriously into moist
   leafy soil   hushes
our happy chatter

a wooden stool
   appears
perched at the edge of a
   still pond
so inviting our feet slow to
   a pause
breathe in sweet mycelial air
   glimpse skyworld
reflected at our toes

A stone wall calls us off trail—built
   by Pocumtuc or Nipmuc?
or white settlers? We listen for the
   stones' story
I read that people of the
   Northern Plains
wore sacred Haploporus odorus beads
   Who remembers
mushroom medicine in this place
   near the Kwinitekw?
Who's harmed by overharvest of
   this good medicine?

Bright orange globs of witch's butter
   tiny white buttons
dusty puff balls, all manner of mushrooms
   magically appear

everywhere.   We walk around
    a decaying tree hosting
patches of jelly and bracket
    fungi. My companion
earth lover and teacher
    points to a dying tree.

"If I were a porcupine I'd be all
    over that nook"
she says, stepping over the
    waterfall beneath.
"You have to let go of any ego
    walking with kids."
Mushroom Matt knows more at
    7 years
old than her at 27.

I spy a tiny, lone,
    red umbrella
mushroom. We gasp in awe, smiles
    wide as skyworld.
When I return let's walk
    in silence
remember these new fungi friends
    vow to listen
more deeply to them and
    their land.

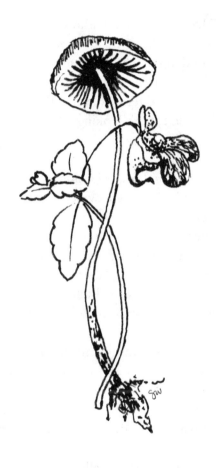

Drawing: Mushroom and Jewelweed

Then and Now
by JuPong Lin

That day they left without me
that day, like so many, I was late,
stood in the gravel lot, uncertain
That day I met Lincoln Fish, tweed-capped
retired forester who wrote the conservation plan.
Both late, both looking
for the same people.

He gestured toward a side path
recently disturbed, evidence they'd passed this way
Further down, evidence of the industry bustling
under these thick woods 300 years ago,
An old road likely built by the First people
who lived in the place now called Indian Hollow
The "natural dam" built by Conwell
not nature's work at all.

That day he warned me before whistling loudly into the wind
We listened for a whistle back,
heard many bird calls
Tufted Titmouse? Black-capped Chickadee?
Birders notice they're migrating north with the shifting climate.

That day we eventually found each other,
the line of colorful hikers
tromping towards us from the other side.

We walk by a huge wall of *Umbilicaria mammulata*
Smooth rock tripe, known to Inuit as famine food,
eaten by starving Continental soldiers at Valley Forge
possibly taught by Oneidas, Tuscaroras,
Mohicans, and the Stockbridge-Munsee Nations
allies to the american revolutionaries.

That day we stopped by the pond and touched the earth

smelled the fertile decomposing leaves
That day before the massacres
in churches, grocery stores, schools
Between that day and the Great Falls massacre 300 years ago
Our feet listen for stories in the ground. At first
all I can hear is grief in the wind.
And then the quiet rustle of oak leaves,
leafy lichen, bright whistle of a Carolina Wren
soothe us, and we find refuge in this
tiny slip of
forest
living long before us humans
and long after
we leave.

Photo: Lichen Rock Tripe

Love Note to the Indian Doctress
by JuPong Lin

before this ridge was staked, named, propertied
by orator, university founder
who named it after himself

in late summer, after vernal pools dry up
and fairy shrimp, salamanders,
wood frogs go under

doctor healer Rhoda Rhoades picked
boneset, goldenrod, sunchoke,
Joe Pye Weed for her "Extract"

her home and many others flooded
by the dam
her plant beings still thrive

webs of worms, feathered ones
nectar sated butterflies
still flutter every spring

PECONIC LAND TRUST

New York

Founded in 1983 by a small group of local residents, Peconic Land Trust conserves Long Island's working farms, natural lands and heritage for our communities now and in the future.

The Trust works with landowners, community groups, partner organizations, donors, and government at all levels to conserve Long Island's agricultural, natural, and cultural resources for all to enjoy and experience. What does this mean:

Fresh local food * Clean drinking water * Healthy water for swimming, kayaking, fishing and shellfishing * Vibrant habitats for plants, birds, and animals * Hiking trails and vistas that enrich the body, mind and soul . . . And so much more!

-Reel Point and Bridge Gardens—Lori Landau
-Smith Corner Preserve and Quail Hill Farm—Scott Chaskey

Peconic Land Trust

Peconic Land Trust works with landowners, community groups, partner organizations, donors, and government at all levels to conserve Long Island's agricultural, natural, and cultural resources for all to enjoy and experience.

For the Trust, *working farms* is an important aspect of our work – in addition to conserving farmland we support the livelihood of farming on Long Island. Through our Farms for the Future Initiative, we are helping new farmers get established as they enter the field. We are leasing and selling protected farmland to both new and established farmers. Acquiring farmland and working with farmers – both new and established – to lease or purchase the land. Providing access to grants and capital improvement programs that assist with equipment and infrastructure improvements and purchases. Providing educational programs, including a well-established apprenticeship program in community supported agriculture (CSA) at our Quail Hill Farm.

Creating climate resilience for our communities is an important focus of our work – by preserving land along shorelines we are providing buffers for storm surge; by working with our local agricultural partners we are ensuring that farmland is available to farmers growing food and giving them the tools and resources to care for the land.

Water, water everywhere. Long Island's sole source aquifer is important to us all . . . protecting the land that sits above the aquifer provides a critical component to ensuring that our drinking water has the space to recharge; and protecting land adjacent to our waterways helps to buffer contaminants from entering our bays, ponds & tributaries, ocean & sound.

Enjoy poems about four of our many conserved lands!

Photos by Peconic Land Trust:
Reel Point-Goldenrod, Beach, Osprey Nest
Bridge Gardens-Sunflower, Herb Garden
Smith Corner-Field
Quail Hill Farm-Gate, Field

Reel Point

I grew up on Long Island and its flowers, herbs and remote waterways run in my blood as cellular memory. Whenever the world is too much for me, I travel back to the shorelines of my youth to soothe myself among the beaches, gardens and woods of Suffolk County. The ancestral lands of the Shinnecock, the Nissequog, and the Manhaset remind me that I am made of the same elements that are found in the trees, seas and wild grasses that are interconnected with my own beingness. The rocky shores of Long Island naturally generate intertidal communities, which are ecosystems found on marine shorelines that are subject to the constant flux of high and low tides. Everything that lives within an intertidal zone—seaweed, crabs, clam, mussels, barnacles, sand dollars, horseshoe crabs, many species of birds and fish and other creatures must be able to survive the radical changes in temperature, salinity, water motion, moisture, wind, and other elements that make up their environment. The poems below reflect the visits I made to the protected areas of the Peconic Land Trust over the course of the spring of 2022, but they also carry a lifetime of felt-sense experiences that are written in-between each line. I was enormously moved by the wild waters that are slowly swallowing the ever-increasing strip of land at Reel Point. It brought back so many memories of long summers spent swimming in the Long Island Sound. The strong smell of fish, cry of the ospreys, feel of the wet stones, and sharp razor clam shells felt so much like home, yet my home ground is at risk of disappearing. Working with land trusts like Peconic, honoring the land through poems is my attempt to help save them. May these poems be in service to the preservation of the many sites that the trust is working to restore for future generations, including Reel Point, and the beautiful Bridge Gardens, both sites which form the foundation and atmosphere of what I've written.

—-Lori Landau
May 2022

Ode to Reel Point
by Lori Landau

Liquid
elemental,
salt on the tongue
of this land
between waters
blue throated howl of tides

primordial pulse
you speak
yet elude language.

your waves could swallow me
if I'm not careful

today,
you are the color of weather
magnificent in your fury.

unnameable beauty
        show me how to find wholeness
in breaking

here is my shattered shell
feather severed from my wings

this is all I have
to give back
to you.

The Osprey of Reel Point
by Lori Landau

Blinking in the sudden light
Pulled upward
buoyed by salt, unafraid
silvery flicker
in somnambulant haze
he swims
just below the surface
unaware of the bird's eye view

everything muffled, quiet
underwater

then,
beat of wings
plunge of feathers above
osprey dives
feet first
the water cushions the blow

the water cushions the blow
feet first
osprey dives
plunge of feathers above
beat of wings
then,
underwater

everything muffled, quiet

unaware of the bird's eye view
he swims
just below the surface
in somnambulant haze
silvery flicker
buoyed by salt, unafraid
pulled upward
blinking in the sudden light

Bridge Gardens
poems by Lori Landau

Bridge Gardens poem 1
(I went to sleep wanting to dream of flowers...

...and dreamed of you,
again,
dying yellow rose.

nothing in this world is permanent
and yet,
this morning at Bridge Gardens,
the fragrance of flowers
fills me with what I need.

those last days,
nothing left to do
but memorize you.

petal, sepal, stem
pistil, bud eye,
bloom —

What has become of you?

is that you in the medicine fields,
dear poppy,
holy basil,
dandelion flung afield?

Filaments afloat   ungraspable

atoms scattered to air

you could be anywhere

☼

Bridge Gardens Dream poem II
(a flower is a bridge)

in a garden
a daffodil,
flower that collects joy,
tips its calix to the sun

The cup of a daffodil is called the trumpet.
the throat of a trumpet is known as the transition.
To "transition" is to go, or cross over.

I have mourned the transience
of honeysuckle, butterfly bushes, lupine

Since you've been gone
I've been writing my dreams
on scraps of paper
that I tie with red thread

let the wind decide
how to carry them

☼

Garden Dream Poem III
(ask the flower)

What a flower knows:
First, the seed
must rupture

ask a flower how to begin
with the wound

Second,
how to shoulder soil

ask a flower how
to break through the dark

how to turn thirst into a mouth
how to bloom despite doubt

a flower can tell you how beauty grows
below the surface

how sacred the roots

walk slowly among flowers
your questions are gods
kneel to them —
iris, lotus, chrysanthemum,

holy sunflower,
that turns its head toward the light.

Shelter Island Sanctuary
by Lori Landau

One

Sea, Sky, Shell. Just

one

Breeze. These day(s),

I need to stand in just

one

place at a time. To hold

one

smooth stone. To be warmed under

one

patch of sun. To slow the loud world down to the call of

one

Piping plover. To be as quiet as

one

flower moth. To become

Like the solitary sandpiper that flies

close to the ground.

As hollow as vertebrae that waves wash through

Or moonlight rising over shimmering waves.

I come to this

one

point

to bow to the sea

To surround myself with the flow

of water. To remember

one

small reason to begin again.

Smith Corner Preserve

Sagaponack
by Scott Chaskey

These reeds I see are full of tears:
        summer rain simplified by grass,
                the pathway of water interrupted by matter.

As it falls the blue heron steps
        through grains of a great web.
                Sand, reeds, rain,

translucent as years,
        water tangible as tears
                on grasses by the salt pond.

Called globes, each orb of rain
        touched by grass, fluid in rest,
         reflects reeds, wings, the surface glitter of summer,
clarity of dwelling in one body.

Quail Hill Farm

Laird at the Croft
by Scott Chaskey

As rough stone
sharpens steel
a man walks

under the hill,
through wet grasses
to tilled field.

Hoe in hand,
hand to wood,
layers of loam sing

rain, sun, leaves
woven with weed—
red root, purslane, lamb's quarters—

and ocean's strong song.
Tool of conduct: hoe.
Hickory shaft

caked with soil
and cool tendrils.
Work. Breathe. Sharpen steel.

Feel this stone
ground to loam
with glacial water.

Woven in grass and silt
a fertile, earthen
intelligence.

Ode
by Scott Chaskey

Downy woodpecker
        flickers in rain
on oak and flesh of grass.

Earth's April flush:
        feathers and thatch.

See in flecks of oakbark
        sun's flame!

The illusive dance
        of earthly transcendence.

BRANFORD LAND TRUST

BRANFORD LAND TRUST

Connecticut

The mission of the Branford Land Trust is to preserve open space in Branford, and to promote our community's appreciation of Branford's diverse natural features.

The Branford Land Trust acknowledges the people who have called the lands we conserve home. We honor the Totoket and Menunkatuck bands of the Quinnipiac people who were dispossessed of these lands. We pay respect to those who are no longer here and we celebrate the continuing and future presence of Indigenous people in this region. We are grateful for their stewardship of land, water, plants, and animals over thousands of years. We also recognize other people – past, present and future – with connections to this land: those who were enslaved and brought here against their will, those who come for a better life, and still others who flee danger and seek refuge. We vow to protect the land in perpetuity, to foster access to nature for all people, and to help heal our human relationship with the earth.

-Beacon Hill—Laurel S. Peterson

Beacon Hill

Traprock ridges, the edges of tilted lava slabs, are one of Connecticut's most distinctive and treasured natural features. Beacon Hill is a 100-foot-high traprock ridge overlooking Long Island Sound and marshes of the Farm River. It is the southernmost summit of the Metacomet Ridge which extends from Long Island Sound north through Connecticut and Massachusetts to nearly the Vermont border.

In addition to offering sweeping water views, the unique microclimates of the Beacon Hill ridge support butterflies, salamanders, and dazzling wildflowers in springtime. The surrounding marsh supports a myriad of wildlife including ospreys, which have made a strong comeback from DDT with the installation of nesting platforms maintained by the Branford Land Trust.

Trails that are open to the public interface with a historic trolley that still carries visitors along an area that was quarried at the turn of the 20th century. The campaign to save Beacon Hill from the threat of development spanned eight years and represented a cooperative partnership between the Branford Land Trust, the Town of Branford, the State of Connecticut, and the public.

Photo: Supply Pond Four Year Old Plays in Puddle by Jan Doyle

Switch grass *Panicum virgatum* by Lauren Brown (pen and ink)

Stony Creek Trolley Trail by Lisa Hesselgrave (oil on canvas)

You Walked With Me Today, Dad
by Laurel S. Peterson

as always on solitary hikes,
your fear for me transferred one afternoon,
when, to teach me to beware,
you dragged me backward
through dirt and leaves in a chokehold.

This morning, I met a couple—
Vermont plates in the parking lot;
their rottweiler demanded
an ear scratch. Later, two older women,
one in an arm cast, paused to watch me
navigate a steep slope.

You weren't wrong: on the news tonight,
another attack in Central Park.
Nowhere is safe, and I admit,
I was almost lost, retracing my steps
through the reeds, up the slope,
choosing the left fork and then the right
before I regained the sure path.

But here in these glorious yellowing woods
edging the salt marsh with its silky
brown-black mud and waving grasses,
the sun needling the water in its game of tag,
I watch black-back gulls circle and land,
finally at rest.

Photo (above): Beacon Hill Trail by Sylvia Ohlrich
Photo (below): Branford Shoreline by Barbara Dwyer

Photo: Supply Pond Thunderhead by Robert Thomas

An Osprey's Vantage Above the Trolley Trail
by Gerry Casanova (graphite sketch)

Tree Near Snake Island
by Carol Cable Hurst (watercolor brush pen)

Turkey Tails
by Laurel S. Peterson

Bittersweet clasps a tree trunk
studded with turkey tail fungi
growing in rows like tabbed file folders.
Mid-afternoon, winter light licks
across the tree like love,
like leaking sap, like an invitation.

What more can we ask for
but the warm smell sunlight releases
from rotting bark?
Or its texture, crumbling beneath our fingers?
Or in this afternoon, while viruses
coach themselves into new forms,
and humans brandish guns at children
and the seas rise while the sky falls,
the one finger pressed against the sharp edges?

Vedders Point by Sharon Hart (watercolor)

Marsh Landing by Sylvia Drewery (watercolour)

Pathway to Pixie-Hoadley Creek by Trish Karter (oil on panel)

Above: Van Wie Woods by Jeanette Mobeck (acrylic)

**Opposite: Juvenile Yellow-Crowned Night Heron
by Maria Stockmal (oil)**

Finding Sanity at Beacon Hill
by Laurel S. Peterson

Winter sunlight crackles off
yesterday's first bright snow
crisscrossed already
with people's tracks.
Five together we wander
carefully six feet apart,
boot toes covered in ice crystals,
exploring the marsh, the lock,
the overlook.

In this moment, there is tolerance
for teenaged beer drinkers,
people with unleashed dogs,
invasive privet.
The paper of daily labor
is muffled, life under snow.

Soon enough, green shoots
will puncture this white carpet.
But in this meditative moment,
only the osprey skreel interrupts,
icing the breeze.

Photo: Early Morning by Tricia Bohan

Photo: Short Beach Preserve by Gaile Ramey

Farm River Morning by Deirdre Baker Schiffer (oil on canvas)

Graffiti
by Laurel S. Peterson

Like the punk rockers at the ecology department party,
you don't fit. Yes, there is human interruption here:
paths, a bench to view the marsh, the lock,
and most egregious, trolley tracks, but
even those somehow suit the aesthetic
of marsh, forest, endless loop of sky.

But you, like discarded beer bottles
or a fire ring, feel a deliberate,
if exuberant, desecration.

Shiny smiling sea monster, green with spiked feet;
giant yellow fish, both with human blue eye,
painted on the lichening rock.
You watch us pass, guardian or
gatekeeper to teenaged dark ritual.
Perhaps you are the future's cave art—
ours is the brilliant eye of a youthful God—
lingering in a corner of dark woods.

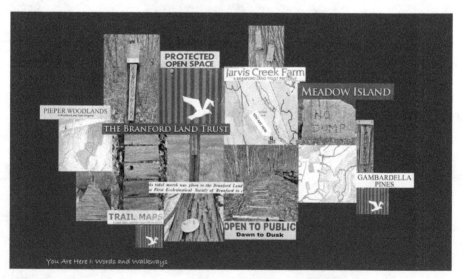

Words and Walkways by Patricia Towle (digital photo collage)

CAPITAL REGION LAND CONSERVANCY

Virginia

The mission of the Capital Region Land Conservancy (CRLC) is to conserve and protect the natural and historic land and water resources of Virginia's Capital Region for the benefit of current and future generations.

-Varina LandLab at Deep Bottom—Maria Elena Scott
-Warwick Road—Gwyn R.C. Moses
-James River Park System—Joanna Lee
-Malvern Hill Farm—Dorinda Wegener

Artist: Katie McBride

About Capital Region Land Conservancy

Created in March 2005 as a non-profit 501(c)3 organization, Capital Region Land Conservancy is the only local land trust serving the Richmond, Virginia area or the "Capital Region." At CRLC, we educate landowners about voluntary land protection tools, facilitate the process of donating conservation easements, and hold conservation easements in perpetuity. CRLC uses a cooperative approach to conservation that balances economic growth with natural resource protection by promoting voluntary land protection and strategic land acquisition to support implementation of local comprehensive plans.

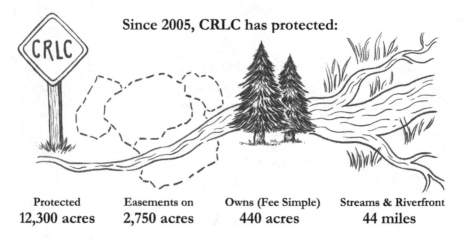

Since 2005, CRLC has protected:

Protected	Easements on	Owns (Fee Simple)	Streams & Riverfront
12,300 acres	**2,750 acres**	**440 acres**	**44 miles**

CRLC is honored to serve an ecologically and culturally diverse region. Farmers, foresters, environmentalists, and everyday lovers of nature come to this work for more reasons than we can count. For our community, the battlefields, historic sites, and sacred grounds we protect offer places to connect, learn about, and process the complicated and often painful history of our region. From acquiring land for local parks to protecting Century Farms, CRLC is committed to ensuring that all communities in our region have access to the outdoors and the land they love.

Whether oak-hickory forests, paw-paw patches, vernal pools, or tidal marshes, our protected lands offer refuge to vulnerable plants and animals in a rapidly changing region. As our land also provides us local food, fresh water, and clean air, we strive to foster communities of care for our people and planet.

Protected Lands of Virginia's Capital Region

Varina LandLab at Deep Bottom – Henrico County, VA

Students have a new classroom at a historic, 350-acre site on the James River and Four Mile Creek. This donated, CRLC-protected land with public access will be utilized by Henrico County Public Schools' Center for Environmental Studies & Sustainability as an experiential learning site. CRLC has since begun to restore forested buffers and native grasslands for ecological health and focus on the important history of the property associated with the Battle of New Market Heights.

Warwick Road – City of Richmond, VA

Donated by the Wilton family in 2020 as a future public park, the 13-acre forested Warwick Road property will provide green space access for over a thousand people in the Deerbourne and Walmsley neighborhoods. Preserving natural green infrastructure in South Richmond supports clean air, clean water, and public park access, while combating urban heat islands in an area impacted by historic racism and systemic inequality. Community needs will guide the future of this park.

James River Park System – City of Richmond, VA

The James River Park System conservation easement, recorded in 2009, was the first of its kind. Perpetual protection of this high traffic, urban park system safeguards approximately 400 acres that host more than 2 million visitors annually. The easement settles concerns that a cash-strapped city might sell off the land for development and ensures stewardship of the natural habitat.

Malvern Hill Farm – Henrico County & Charles City County, VA

In February 2018, CRLC purchased the 871-acre Malvern Hill Farm for $6.5 million. Located along historic Route 5, the property was the site of a 17th century manor and plantation that witnessed troops during the American Revolution, War of 1812, and Civil War. Most notably was the bloody battle fought on July 1, 1862. After transferring 428 acres to Henrico County for a future park under a conservation easement, in 2022 CRLC transferred the remaining 371 acres to the National Park Service, Richmond National Battlefield Park.

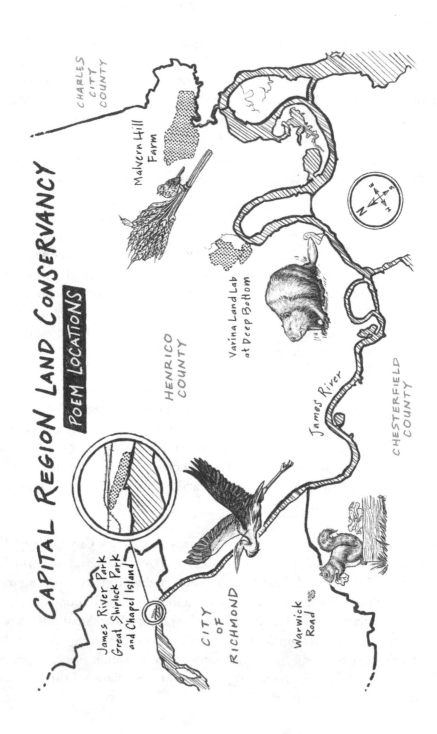

Varina LandLab at Deep Bottom

Bless Us, Mamá Earth
  -With special thanks to Rudolfo Anaya
by Maria Elena Scott

Let us bless this land

For all students and educational leaders
That they may know the treasures that it holds

For the workers who will conserve and restore it
That they may feel pride in a dream well dreamt

Let us sanctify this place

For future generations
That they may know the history of the Civil War battles fought

That they may ponder the cost of war

Let us make holy the 353 acre preserve
For the flora and the fauna that exists there

That they may not only live but thrive in their many habitats

Let us vow to enjoy this newly named area
Without disturbing the landscape for Mamá Earth

Let us all rejoice at her many wonders

Mamá Earth Speaks
by Maria Elena Scott

Keep me safe
From the high rise towers of progress

For the beaver who leaves
tell tale chips of his industrious ways

Keep me safe
For the young pine trees that add
Beauty to my face

For the sweet gum, silver maple
River birch and redbud trees

For the amber waves of broom sage
That provide shelter to migratory birds

Keep me safe
For the blue stem, river oats and soft rush grasses
Which dance with the Western Wind

Keep me safe
From the high rise towers of progress
For our children's children

Keep me safe

Visiting Varina Earthlab
by Maria Elena Scott

In the always opened arms of Mamá Earth
Warblers tweet their morning salutation
Tiny mustard yellow flowers at my feet

Two headstones mark
The remains of mother and son

A rifle pit where Civil War soldiers dug in
Defensive shooting positions

Pillows of small white chokeberry
Dot the landscape symmetry

A pair of wild turkeys
Cross the one lane road

Five foot tall amber waves of broom sage
As far as the eye can see

A cool breeze changes direction
Caressing my face

At the edge of the historic James River

Warwick Road

Trees Foretell the Measure of War
by Gwyn R.C. Moses

Tree heights push concealment of graves much deeper.
Train rails shiver between burly trunks.
Swift boxcars screech lingering melodies.
Tree muscles uphold vibrant headdresses.
Birds whistle and squirrels chatter between shining leaves.
Tender woods gather bottomless roots.
Mighty dark limbs bend.
Bleak odors expel.
Meek stems droop.
Flowers diminish.
Brisk winds sway revering and cursing.
Like soldiers in formation, trees grieve horrific tales.
Height of trees can be seen way down the road.
Posturing to defend passing turmoil.
On guard to collapse modernistic views.
Roots pinned together soak journeys of angry souls.
The fallen we will never come to know.
The height of the trees is the height of war.

The Greenway
by Gwyn R. C. Moses

I stand alone in the midst of her watching.
I stand alone in the midst of her wondering.
Oh! So scented.
Yet, no flowers.
Footprints remain of trampling.
Moist piles of fertile soil are scraped.
The man steers a shaky roaring tractor.
Its blade is held up before the knife slices.
Ridding any evidence of flowering.
Piercing beeps call upon the sheathable.
As if pain is remedy.
Hallowing out love, a blue marble, and china doll's arm.
Once hidden as lucky charms.

Will she laugh again?

The plot is tossed.
Like casual lovers under silk threads.
I stand nearby.
Leaning on a wise tree.
Squirrels nibble garden plants delicately.
Waiting for Spring to turn brittle grass into summer dust.
I stand nearby.
Weeping and smiling.
Reincarnated soil mourns.
Until
the
new
playground
is
constructed.

A nature trail will run the same course.
Consume life with shared pathology.

James River Park System:
Chapel Island and Great Shiplock Park

Haibun for an island that is no longer an island
by Joanna Lee

There are many paths down to the water. On spring days like this one, even the sky drips, whispering the greens of summer into wet existence. What were you called before you were weighted with the hardness of hewn stone? Was it a summer name, fluid, draped with a skin of stars? Was it made of all a river can know of language—words for every shade of life that tiptoes roots into the cradle of her bed? Did you sing back with the joy of your silences, the flutter and crawl and stamp of time? On spring days like this, did you share a tongue, the tug of warm mud where one nature holds the hand of another, passing secrets in the slow burst of a bead of honeysuckle?

The river hums a different song now, maybe. Colder, more lonely. She has seen more sadness lapping at your edges than even the rain can wash clean. Maybe you remember. Maybe you have taught yourself to choose to forget. To us who never learned to shape our ears around the syllables of earth and current, or to dance in the rhythms that lie outside of rhythm, there is only mystery, and regret.

And yet there is laughter: in the sinking of graffitied cement into your riots of vine, bright colors swallowing bright colors until wild strawberries cover all, your heart closing like a fist content. If we who are deaf to such things could translate the crank of the heron overhead, it might say *let go*.

foam swirls from cold pipe
and smiles in snake-like knowing
as it becomes still

Study of a shoreline
by Joanna Lee

The quiet of a place
that cannot decide
if it wants to be forgotten
will always breathe with ghosts

Ghosts of ships that were never put to sea,
with their ring of ghostly hammers
on sullen metal slunk into the rain's
steady echo

Ghosts of the fishermen
who took from these currents
their brothers in sandy pools; ghosts
of lure and line and old bones

In the wet rust of leaf fall, ghosts
of patient towpath oxen
& great weighted bateaus
drug through one canal chamber to the next

Ghosts
of all those boats carried,
from the city and back to her;
ghosts of a future that was to meet them at the docks

Ghosts, too, of iron and creosote, of ice blocks
and pickaxes and bibles. You can see their pale hands
when breeze off the river blows the Queen Anne's lace
just so

Ghosts of beginnings, and of hope, tried prayers
in a new tongue, how they grew
into the stale ghosts
of smoke, again and again

Under all, the ghosts of waters that knew this land
like a lover, before the river fell and the bay drew back,
a lament that drips through the long-closed canal locks
like a live thing, remembering

Driving the river roads at night, close on Chapel Isle
by Joanna Lee

tracks
loom out of a black nowhere: the break

in the floodwall, arcing over asphalt to span
lofts still stained with tobacco-leaf

and canal, orphan- & slave-built super-
highway of a dream. Who prayed here,

knees in salty mud,
in the dawns before

they raised a church up on the Hill?
Did they find peace in the reflected shallows

rock-skips from Richmond Dock,
so much unloaded from the water?

Who sought forgiveness? Who miracles?
Whose faith was lost when the flour mills burned

alongside the shipyards?
A city left

sorting its laundry from stormwaste
whose dirty secrets are kept from the river

with the weight of cement. Rail's draw-
bridge long welded shut, wet tar

stains still the skin of young palms
who come fishing for redemption,

lured by that which is still holy.

Malvern Hill Farm

Reflections on Wheat: A Prayer in Four Parts
    –Malvern Hill Farm, VA
by Dorinda Wegener

I

Goats were pouring forth their pure milk.
Anemones were piercing the road's ribs.
Lice were biting the seers gathered in gawk.
Almonds were blanching in bowls of cruor.
Teeth were breaking gum or falling out.
Breath was fouling close to necks, to ears.
Tongues were separating themselves.
Houses were massing their shadow's length.
Letters were uniting into lenten plots.
      Who do you believe me to be?
          Is not the same as
                Who do you say that I am?

A gravel path raked by death dragging
      is the same as a bloom
            on the staff of life.

II

Wheat grass covers the field
where once switchblade and broom
sage grew, big and little
blue stem, wild rye–the word *preserve*
in Late Latin means *'to keep /*
in advance of' coming rows,
soft red winter, your brother:
an ancient grain, our ancestors,
roots not native to this soil.

III

The devil hath desired to sift us as wheat.
Tillers and mainstem cut down: sickle, then scythe
then reaper-binder, the wheat flail working
loose the berries, the wind awhistle through
the straw as the sparrow shrieks.

IV

This land, before fallow field or cultivated crop,
before stolen and bloodshed, before we
forced our own history upon it, before
we faithfully answered, *Who do you believe me to be,*
before our weaknesses were revealed in the winnowing
and we falsely witnessed, *Who do you say that I am,*
let us relearn Latin, relearn, as in *conserve*
'to keep / together,' may the land take us to breast,
may the land carry us under her arm, as if
we were omers of wheat to sieve
and knead into a rough hewn boule—
　　　　may the land leave us out to prove,
　　　　　　may we rise, together, by grace.

After the Prescribed Fire
by Dorinda Wegener

It has been a long time: this field
reclaimed by cedar saplings, bone

roots cross under earthworks once singed,
savanna-like pines still stand, heat

hollowed, whose perches couch a tawny plume
–lone hawk's cypher eyes do rove

talon tally down to woodland vole.
          Here is the morning wake: this sunrise

successional, stage of red, a sash
athwart an ember breast, withered

wreath with ribbons tressed, now littered
days, lorn, and rust, in truss my heart

with grief, the simple loss of us.

PROSPECT PARK

New York City

Prospect Park Alliance is the non-profit organization that sustains, restores and advances Prospect Park, "Brooklyn's Backyard," in partnership with the City of New York. The Alliance was founded in 1987 to help restore the Park after a long period of deterioration and decline. Today, the Alliance provides critical staff and resources that keep the Park green and vibrant for the diverse communities that call Brooklyn home. The Alliance cares for the woodlands and natural areas, restores the Park's buildings and landscapes, creates innovative Park destinations, and provides volunteer, education and recreation programs. Prospect Park is one of Brooklyn's most treasured destinations with more than 10 million visits each year. Learn more at www.prospectpark.org.

-Poets:
- -Michaeline Picaro
- -Opalanietet
- -Rachelle Parker

ReImagine Lefferts Initiative

The Alliance is undertaking *Writing the Land* as part of its *ReImagine Lefferts* initiative.

Lefferts Historic House is an 18th-century Flatbush, Brooklyn, farmhouse and a New York City landmark, which is jointly operated by Prospect Park Alliance and the Historic House Trust. The farmhouse was originally located just a few blocks from the park in the village of Flatbush, and beginning with Lefferts family member Pieterse van Hagewout, five generations resided in the Lefferts home and farm. One can trace the Lefferts' wealth to the labor of enslaved African people and servants that enabled the family to live a comfortable and profitable existence. Enslaved Africans worked the lands that comprised the Lefferts family farm to produce staple crops starting in the late 1600s.

The farmhouse moved to Prospect Park in 1917, and became a historic house museum. The museum features period rooms, indoor and outdoor exhibits, historic artifacts, reproductions and working farm plots. Through hands-on experiences, cultural performances, and imaginative play, visitors learn about the rich history of Brooklyn and also gather together to celebrate the diversity of our community today.

The Alliance has launched *ReImagine Lefferts* to re-envision the mission and programming of the museum to recognize its role as a site of slavery, and tell the stories—in innovative, inclusive and forward-thinking ways—of the enslaved Africans and the Indigenous people of the Lenapehoking who lived and worked the land. As the Alliance reimagines the mission of the museum, we seek to engage the public in a thoughtful dialogue about the legacy of slavery and the treatment of marginalized communities who have contributed to the rich tapestry of Brooklyn. Learn more at www.prospectpark.org/lefferts.

Photo: Lefferts Historic House by Prospect Park Alliance

Map by Prospect Park Alliance

Photo: Winter © Martin Seck

INDIAN VILLAGES
PATHS, PONDS
AND PLACES
IN
KINGS COUNTY

Walk a mile in another's moccasins you say,
trails of red chronicled on an aged map of Brooklyn.

Stained with footsteps of ancestors long ago,
reduced to a line in history, noting Indian trails here.

Stained and yellow like parchment of the past,
Seal our chapter and dust the specimen jar.

Commence perceptuality in pen and ink with noun decree,
"Trails that exist today as major thoroughfares,like Fulton Street,
Flatbush Avenue, and part of Atlantic Avenue"! mandating
everlasting contribution of a thousand footsteps.

Opposing yellow parchment and red ink dictation,
sprightly moccasins with spirit and praises to all creations.
Ceremonies with heart and song for creators' gifts of mother
earth, grandfather stone, grandmother moon, grandfather tree,
they have shown us the way.

Our footprints dissolve inanimation, yellowing parchment and
red ink encased in tomb,
Munsee children have not forgotten ancestor's gait, treading
lightly on path, prayer on lips,
Ceremony, teachings of heart, ancestors are lively and spry
within spirit, stone, tree, and trail.

Manitou footsteps, my ancestors are flourishing and vital, living
in our teachings and DNA, they are still here, we are still here,
Ramapough Munsee Lunaape, we have not forgotten.

---by Michaeline Picaro

We are still here
by Michaeline Picaro

We are still here.
Not all are tucked away like parks in cities.
Close- knit, core communities and dispersed afar in cities block.
Outdated History needs correction, NY, NJ, CT, MA, RI, we are still here.
Cities subjugate nature into insignificant pockets, it is still here.
Minuscule compared to its former honor, tucked away awaiting the unexpected wanderer.
They visit, enjoy or study, unearthing teachings of heart and spirit.
Nature is still here. We are still here, with teachings of heart and spirit.
We Native Americans are synergistic, onto parks of nature.
We are not gone, we are Resilience!
One of many Nations, Ramapough Lenape Nation
We are still here.

Photo: Long Meadow © Martin Seck

Photo: Fall Biking © Martin Seck

Hearing Birds
by Opalanietet

Sirens, horns, trains, the heat

Cool, enclosed green interior...relief.
Stroll...think...tingling breeze
The most enjoyable...peaceful...almost sneeze

Oak...sycamore...maple
Kids enjoying games...laughing...by a picnic table
People...citizens...perambulate...and smile

Wail of siren, emergency, going to be late — hurry up!

Split...cracked...pavement of the sidewalk
Attempted...taming of the wild...is the Earth trying to talk?

Please...squirrel...don't hurry...so fast
We...need...this...serenity...to last

The scurrying reminds me — what am I doing? Have things to do!

Birds...chirping...okay...playful robin redbreast
Peace...is at hand...birds singing...is a test.

When birds...don't sing...often means...a predator is near
Music abounds...the Earth is happier...there is no fear

What time is it? Head for exit. Have to leave.
Concrete, street lights, back in element — nothing to fear
Wait! I hear no birds. Is a predator near?

Free Land Exists in Brooklyn
by Opalanietet

A land birthed free, sculpted by Creator
Utilization of ice pick, remnants of glacial ridge still seen
This land that still is Lenapehoking.

We give thanks to the Marechkawieck, we give thanks to the Canarsee
Which without their stewardship, this oasis never could have been
This land that still is Lenapekhoking.

Freedom is to roam, freedom is to play, freedom is to choose to stay
To be free with this land, we have no landlord, we have no king, or queen
This land that still is Lenapehoking.

Stolen, divided, quarantined for privatized use
Reconfigured, reimagined, a public space so green

This land that still is Lenapehoking.

Photo: Lakeside © Martin Seck

Photo: Fall Lake © Martin Seck

The Mommas, The Daddies, Us Kids…We Together
by Rachelle Parker

While the Mommas are helped by
the Daddies over the stone wall, us kids
had already ran and found the tree
with the big roots and lots of shade
and low branch to throw a sheet over
in case some of us needed privacy
to change our popsicle-stained clothes.

We put our pails out as borders
for our family blankets. We wait,
playing hand games and musical
rocks, jumping on stones, never
leaving one empty. We see that big
old lake and hear the carousel
and know it's over there somewhere.

Then we see our parents, our
Mommas wearing halter tops
and cotton wrap skirts and our
Daddies in their short sleeve
dress shirts and plaid shorts,
hauling the grill and charcoal
and the cooler full of ice chilling
C&C sodas. A shopping cart rolls
along with hamburger buns, hot
dog buns, a loaf of white bread
for bologna sandwiches or to wrap
around a fried chicken leg or thigh,
the badminton rackets and birdie
and net, a grocery store ball, swirly
orange. Skates. The kind that fasten
to your shoes. A woven basket
on top holding the dishes of baked
beans, potato salad and cucumbers
with vinegar, salt and pepper.

The Mommas and Daddies are
so young. Gram and Pop too.
The men strong, The women
still with a wiggle in their step.

And you wonder if the good
grasses of the park know
that the Mommas have passed
on and left us kids to continue without
them. Will these good grasses
remind us to be careful when
we play and to have a seat
out the sun for a minute
and to go over by the Daddies?

Will these good grasses, that our Mommas
ran their feet through, tell us things
on picnic day?

Photo: Spring in Prospect Park © Martin Seck

Photo (above): White Levy Esplanade © Martin Seck
Photo (below): Path © Martin Seck

A Damselfly Is Not A Lady Dragonfly
by Rachelle Parker

They are their own kind.
Gliding across lakes. With their
own moms and dads, children.
Pretty. Wings iridescent. Knitted.
Delicate. Filigree. Whizzing
between boys and girls with
popsicles whose own wings are knotted
under skin the color of rasped
nutmeg wait to unfurl, soar,
catch sun, become heart
shaped and moms and dads with children,
dart, scuffle, stay safe
and alive amidst the genus,
amidst the skittishness.

Photo: Lake © Martin Seck

Photo: Grand Army Plaza © Martin Seck

FLUSHING MEADOWS CORONA PARK

New York City

Flushing Meadows Corona Park, located in Queens, is one of the five largest parks in New York City. It was founded on the original site of the 1939/'40 and 1964/'65 World's Fairs. Today, the public can enjoy birding, hiking, strolling, picnics, boating, and sports year-round. Honored with the nickname "The World's Park" due to its location in the most diverse community in the country, the park serves as everyone's "backyard," offering free movies under the stars, outdoor fitness classes, playgrounds, athletic fields for cricket, soccer and baseball, and heritage festivals.

The Alliance for Flushing Meadows Corona Park, the park's nonprofit partner, supports NYC Parks to preserve, maintain, and improve Flushing Meadows Corona Park for the benefit and use of the surrounding communities and all New Yorkers.

As stewards, we aspire to raise awareness and engage the community by caring for the natural environment, preserving our history, and providing exceptional amenities and programming. We are committed to making the park accessible for all to enjoy, now and for future generations. Together, we make it all it can be for the public, wildlife, and the environment.

-Poets: Grisel Y. Acosta & Kimiko Hahn
-English Translators: Grisel Y. Acosta (Spanish, all poems); Chen Yihai 义海 (Chinese for Acosta's poems); Zhang Ziqing 张子清 (Chinese for Hahn's poems)

there is a nest
after the Unisphere Red-Tailed Hawks
by Grisel Y. Acosta

there is a nest
atop a globe of shiny steel
where a mother cares for her young
undaunted by the man-made metal cage
focused on the fledgling child
who will one day leap outside
the sphere, fly beyond
soar high above and see
how small it looks

hay un nido
después de los halcones de cola roja del Unisfera
escrito y traducido por Grisel Y. Acosta

hay un nido
encima de un globo de acero brillante
donde una madre cuida a sus crías
impávida por la jaula de metal hecha por hombre
enfocada en el volantón
quien un día saltará afuera
de la esfera, volará más allá,
se elevará en alto para ver
que pequeñita se ve

那里有一只鸟巢
——跟踪公园里地球仪雕塑上的红尾鹰
格里塞尔·Y. 阿科斯塔

有一只鸟巢
在那闪亮的钢铁的地球仪雕塑的顶上
一只母鹰在那里呵护她的孩子
她根本不在乎这人造的金属的笼子
专心致志地呵护她羽毛未丰的孩子
有一天这孩子会腾空而出
飞出这地球仪，飞向远方
在高空翱翔俯视大地
并发现这地球仪是那么小

when a wish is a park
for Vincent
by Grisel Y. Acosta

I see you on your balcony
watching the kids run toward Corona
to the silver center that you imagine as
a piece of the Milky Way brought down
like a mercury comet landing in your 'hood

you thought it was just a space to run
free and maybe make a friend that would
take you away from the confines of harsh
religion that said no to celebrations of any kind
a place to fantasize about another world

you knew nothing of the boats,
the music propelling limbs into windmills,
or vendors selling corn spiced with jalapeños and
sweets made of tamarindo and guayaba,
least of all the rocket, sized exactly for a child

it was as though your own feet became jet-fueled
thrusters lifting your body into the air that day
when your eyes first saw the model, and then
your heart both rose and sank in a gravity of confusion
wishing you'd seen this when you were a locked-up kid,

yet grateful that you were seeing it now with me,
and I felt the same, wanting your younger self to have
that moment of elation, and praising the gift of seeing
you walk towards the spaceship that made you squeal,
"What? There's a rocket in Corona Park?"

un parque es un sueño
para Vincent
escrito y traducido por Grisel Y. Acosta

te veo en tu balcon
viendo a los niños correr hacia Corona
gravitando al centro plateado que imaginas es
un pedazo de la Vía Láctea que ha caído
como un cometa de mercurio, aterrizando en tu barrio

pensaste que era solo un espacio para correr
libre y tal vez hacer un amigo que te
sacaría de los confines de religión dura
que te nego celebraciones de cualquier tipo
un lugar para fantasear de otro mundo

ni siquiera sabías de los barcos,
la música que impulsaba las piernas de breakdancers en molinos
de viento, o de vendedores de elotes con jalapeños y
dulces hechos de tamarindo y guayaba,
menos que nada el cohete, del tamaño exacto para un niño

fue como si tus propios pies se convirtieron en chorros,
propulsores levantando tu cuerpo en el aire ese día
cuando tus ojos vieron por primera vez el modelo, y luego
tu corazón se elevó y se hundió en una gravedad de confusión
deseando haber visto esto cuando eras un niño encerrado,

pero agradecido de que lo estabas viendo ahora conmigo,
y sentí lo mismo, queriendo que el "tú" más joven tuviera
ese momento de euforia, y alabando el don de verte
caminar hacia la nave espacial que te hizo chillar,
"¿Qué *qué*? ¿Hay un cohete en Corona Park?"

当愿望是一座公园
——献给文森特
格里塞尔·Y. 阿科斯塔

我看到你在阳台上
看着孩子们奔向科罗娜公园
跑向白银中心，而在你看来
它就像银河落入人间的一部分
就像一颗闪亮的彗星落在你的头巾上

你觉得那是一个可以奔跑的地方
无拘无束，或许还可以交到朋友
使你摆脱严苛的宗教的束缚
据说在宗教里不得有任何庆祝
那是个幻想另一个世界的地方

你对船可是一无所知，
不知道音乐驱动四肢变成风车
也不认识贩卖的、洒了辣椒粉的爆米花
或者那些用奇异水果制成的糖果
更不用说火箭：它的大小正好适合孩子。

你的双脚像是注了燃料推进器似的
那一整天你的身体都好像是腾空了
当你第一次见到那个模型，然后
你的心因为阵阵慌乱而起伏，希望
自己还是个封闭少年时就已见过这些，

谢天谢地，你现在与我一起都看到了这些
我也感到很庆幸，真希望年轻时的你
拥有这份喜悦，并为有这眼福而赞美
你走向那艘宇宙飞船，它让你尖叫起来：
"天哪！科罗娜公园里居然有一个火箭？"

(free) form
by Grisel Y. Acosta

even though we live on this land
there is no formal sign of us in this park, until
we get to a corner surrounded by rose bushes
a silver U high on a black monolith
created by someone called "de Rivera"
familiarly named like my sister-in-law
we celebrate that there is a Latinx sculptor
featured, wishing we had known sooner

"The Colonial Disease does result in non-
existence, death and dismemberment,
orphaning, alienation and wounding….because
many of us are now a people of mixed-blood-
and-culture, we must balance
fragmented and divided identities."

there are many parallels between
de Rivera and myself: he was born a
September Virgo, liked handiwork,
hung out at the Art Institute of Chicago
liked to travel, drink, smoke weed…
we could have been friends in another
universe but for my race—see, this free-
spirit began on a plantation—another
seeming parallel, but his engineer father was paid

so now, I must revise my feelings
once again, like when I went to get pierced
and the woman behind the counter said, "My mom
loved my ex-boyfriend, a Dominican, but she
said, 'You know you're going to have Black babies'"
did she say this despite my being there or because of it?

Corona Park on a Sunday is a euphony of
Japanese, Spanish, Mandarin, Russian,

disco, hip hop, freestyle, classical, soul
bird calls, squeals of children, bells of elote vendors
and wind swooping through leaves, flags, and metal
bent into the shapes of the world

my lover and I so wanted to feel
represented by this Spaniard, desiring
a name in stone to, just for once, be ours,
someone who came from our neighborhood,
a carving making the history we know permanent,
but these Spanish names are just as foreign
as the English—what are our real names,
our real spaces and places, after all?

de Rivera traveled to Cuba, Spain,
Egypt, Turkey, Italy, learned engineering
from his father, his art from the masters
of his craft, an international web of
men (not much is said about his mom)
his Smithsonian interviewer stated, "It
sounds like a very easy, very free…"
He said, "I was free. I had no particular
schedule." I say, "That must be nice."

we freely roam the park
reminisce about the "Mundos
Alternos" exhibit at the Queens Museum
unaware that the original design
for the Unisphere "accidentally
left off Puerto Rico" and other
locations with people of color

a Barbabos-born dancer pirouettes
like a god holding up the Unisphere
for a Wall Street Journal article which
explains that his family didn't want
him to dance at carnaval because of gun
violence; ballet is depicted as his savior

Robert Moses wanted a hierarchy
of lights for the Unisphere, with larger
blue bulbs for "more important nations"
African American planning committee
members argued against this plan, citing
a "questionable psychology"–ultimately,
all illuminations were created equally

I was born free and I am free
so, I see these spaces as remnants
of old ideas that have been taken
over by the baile of languages
and people who will always reinvent
stone and steel into what suits them
whether it is a yoga class for older women
or a Trinidadian birthday party, this sphere
will twist and turn to the form of its current
creators—we make our fragments one starlight

References/Referencias/ 参考 :

Campanella, Thomas J. "Icon of a Fair, a Borough, the World." 11 Sept. 2010. *The Wall Street Journal.*

Catton, Pia. "Cruising Through Art of the Caribbean." 22 July 2012. *The Wall Street Journal.*

Cummings, Paul. "Oral history interview with José de Rivera, 1968, February 24." *Smithsonian Institute.*

"De Rivera, José Ruiz, 1904-1985." *Social Networks and Archival Content.* snaccooperative.org.

Provost, M.C.L. and Quintana, M. "Unbodies of water: The health effects of extinction and genocide — Arawak perspectives." *American Psychological Association.* Aug. 2010.

(forma) libre
traducido y escrito por Grisel Y. Acosta

aunque vivamos en esta tierra
no hay ninguna señal formal de nosotros en este parque,
hasta que llegamos a una esquina rodeada de rosales
una U plateada en lo alto de un monolito negro
creado por alguien llamado "de Rivera"
familiarmente llamado como mi cuñada
celebramos que haya un escultor latino
presente, deseando haberlo sabido antes

> "La Enfermedad Colonial resulta en no-
> existencia, muerte y desmembramiento,
> orfandad, enajenación y herida….porque muchos
> de nosotros somos ahora un pueblo de sangre
> mixta-y-cultura, debemos equilibrar
> identidades fragmentadas y divididas".

> Hay muchos paralelismos entre
> de Rivera y yo: nació un Virgo de
> Septiembre, le gustaba la artesanía, pasamos
> el rato en el Instituto de Arte de Chicago.
> le gustaba viajar, beber, fumar hierba…
> podríamos haber sido amigos en otro
> universo pero…mi raza—mira, este espíritu
> libre comenzó en una plantación, otro paralelo,
> aparentemente, pero a su padre ingeniero le pagaban

así que ahora, debo revisar mis sentimientos
una vez más, como cuando fui a un salón de tatuajes
y la mujer detrás del mostrador dijo: "Mi mamá
amaba a mi exnovio, un dominicano, pero ella
dijo: 'Sabes que vas a tener bebés negros'".
¿Dijo esto a pesar de que estaba allí o porque estaba allí?

> Corona Park en domingo es una eufonía de
> japonés, español, mandarín, ruso,

discoteca, hip hop, freestyle, clásicas, soul,
cantos de pájaros, chillidos de niños, campanas
de vendedores de elote y el viento atravesando hojas,
banderas y metal doblado en las formas del mundo

mi amante y yo queríamos tanto sentir
representados por este español, deseando
un nombre en piedra que, por una vez, era cerca
a lo nuestro, alguien que vino de nuestro barrio,
un tallado que hiciera permanente la historia que conocemos,
pero los nombres españoles son igualmente extranjeros
que los ingleses, ¿cuáles son nuestros verdaderos nombres,
nuestros espacios y lugares auténticos, después de todo?

de Rivera viajó a Cuba, España,
Egipto, Turquía, Italia, aprendió ingeniería
de su padre, su arte de los maestros
de su oficio, una red internacional de
hombres (no se habla mucho de su mamá)
su entrevistador del Smithsonian declaró:
"Suena como algo muy fácil, muy libre…"
Él dijo: "Yo era libre. No tenia calendario."
Yo digo: "Eso debe ser agradable"….

deambulamos libremente por el parque
recordamos la exposición "Mundos Alternos"
en el Museo de Queens sin saber que el diseño
original para el Unisfera "accidentalmente
dejo Puerto Rico afuera del diseño" y, por supuesto,
otros lugares con gente privado de derechos

un bailarin nacido en Barbados hace piruetas
como un dios sosteniendo el Unisfera
en un artículo del Wall Street Journal que
explica que su familia no quería que
él bailara en el carnaval por violencia armada;
el ballet representa su salvador, según el artículo

Robert Moses quería una jerarquía
de luces para el Unisfera, con bombillas
azules mayores para "naciones más importantes"
miembros afroamericanos del comité de planificación
se opusieron a este plan, citando una "psicología
cuestionable" - en última instancia, todas las
iluminaciones fueron creadas en tallas iguales

Nací libre y soy libre entonces,
veo estos espacios como remanentes
de ideas viejas que han sido sustituidas
por un baile de lenguas y gente
que siempre reinventarán piedra
y acero en lo que les conviene, si es
una clase de yoga para mujeres mayores
o una fiesta de cumpleaños trinitense, esta esfera girará
y girará a la forma de su creadoras actuales:
hacemos de nuestros fragmentos una luz estelar

自由体
格里塞尔·Y.阿科斯塔

我们虽然生活在这片土地上
但在这个公园里并无特别的标志显示
忽然，当我们来到一处被玫瑰簇拥的拐角时
才发现在一块黑色磐石上有个银色的"U"
那是一个叫"德·里维拉"的人的作品
这名字看上去很熟悉像我的弟媳的名字
我们 庆幸 这里专有一个拉丁风格的雕塑家
要是我们早就知道就更好了

> "殖民地病确实导致毁灭
> 死亡和分离，流离失所，
> 导致疏远和伤害……因为
> 我们现代人现在都是混合血统的
> 文化的人，我们应该平衡
> 我们碎片化和分裂的身份。"

德·里维拉和我之间有很多
相似之处：他是出身在九月
是处女座，喜欢手工艺
在芝加哥艺术学院鬼混
喜欢旅行，喝酒，抽烟叶…
因为种族的缘故，在另一个世界
我们本可以是朋友——你瞧，这种
自由精神开始于种植园——这好像是
另一个相似点，而他工程师的父亲却得了好处。

所以现在，我必须重新修正我的
感觉，就像我去给耳朵打孔时那样
只听得柜台后面的女人说："我妈妈
很喜欢我的前男友，一个多米尼加人，但她
又说，'你知道你会生下一个黑婴儿的'"
她是不是故意说给我听的呢？

星期天的科罗娜公园像一首和谐乐曲：
日语、西班牙语、普通话、俄语
迪斯科、街舞、自由舞、古典舞
鸟鸣、孩子的叫声、烤玉米小贩的铃铛声……
风呼呼地吹过树叶，旗帜，还有
金属弯曲成这个世界的形状

我的爱人和我于是有一种感觉，希望
这个西班牙人是我们的代表，渴望
刻在石头里的名字，哪怕一次，就是我们的，
这样我们群体中就有人的名字刻在那里，
这样雕塑就会让我们所知道的历史成为永恒，
可是这些西班牙的名字跟英语里的名字一样
都是外来的——什么才是我们真正的名字？
再说，我们的世界和整个世界又是什么呢？

德·里维拉曾游历过古巴、西班牙
埃及、土耳其、意大利，从他父亲那里
学习了工程学，从他这一行的各种大师那里
学习了他的技艺，那可以一种
跨越国界的人脉（对他母亲则只字未提）
史密森学会的记者说："听他讲话
感觉他非常放松，非常自在……"
他说："我是毫无拘束的。我没有特定的
日程。"我说："那一定很美妙。"

我们漫不经心地在公园里走着
回味着在皇后博物馆里的
"世界之光"的展览
并未在意公园里"地球仪"
原初的设计"偶然将
波多黎 哥 漏掉了"，包括
其他一些有色人种的地区

一个巴巴多斯出身的舞者踮着脚尖起舞
他像一个神似的托起地球仪
为《华尔街日报》的一篇文章插图
这篇文章写道，他的家人不愿意

在狂欢节上跳舞是因为担心枪支
暴力；并说，芭蕾就是他的救赎

　　　　　　罗伯特·摩西本来要为"地球仪"设计
　　　　　　具有等级制的照明系统，给那些
　　　　　　"更重要的国家"用更大的蓝色灯泡
　　　　　　非裔美国人计划委员会成员
　　　　　　反对这个计划，认为
　　　　　　这是一种"值得讨论的心理"——最终
　　　　　　所有的照明等便设计得大小一样了

我生来自由，我是自由的
所以，我在这些空间里看到
旧观念的残余，而这些观念
已经被各种语言和人们取代
而他们总是将石头和金属
塑造成适合他们需要的形状
不管是老太太们的一堂瑜伽课
还是一场特立尼达的生日派对
这个"地球仪"都会扭曲以适合
当下创造者的模样——我们则将我们的碎片化作一束星光

Ode to the Rushes in Flushing Meadows Corona Park
by Kimiko Hahn

Thankfully, neither grass nor lawn
you are startled browns
holding on to the water's ledge where
I measure my self worth
with how purely I become you:
the winter wind zizzing through
then calming in a ruffled quiet
but for the water's lap lap lapping,
but for the plane's roar
over Unisphere to tarmac. You are
the present without tension,
a gift for the moment. I thank you.

Oda a los Junqueros del Prado Flushing/Parque Corona
por Kimiko Hahn

Agradecidamente, ni hierba ni césped,
son marrones sorprendidos
aguantándose a la repisa del agua donde
mido mi autoestima
con mi habilidad pura en conventirme en tí:
el viento de invierno zizzando entre todo
y entonces calmandose en un alborotado tranquilidad
a menos del lapea, lapea, lapeando del agua
a menos del rugido de avion
sobre Unisfera hasta la pista. Tú eres
el presente sin tensión,
un regalo del momento. Te doy gracias.

法拉盛草甸科罗娜公园的灯心草颂
吉米柯 · 哈恩

值得庆幸的是，既不是草也不是草坪，
你是受惊的灯心草，
抓着水面的礁石，在那里，
我用我同你一样的纯粹
来衡量我的自我价值：
冬天的风呼啸而过，
然后在一片喧闹的宁静中平静下来，
除了海水的拍打，
除了飞机在巨型地球雕塑 上空
呼啸着飞向停机坪。
你是自然 而，
是当下的礼物。谢谢你。

Ode to the Air in Flushing Meadows Corona Park
by Kimiko Hahn

Framed by the Van Wyck, the Grand Central,
Union Turnpike, and Meadow Lake—
you waft and chill. You open to all
in every weather. You carry the exhaust
and buzz of traffic over a clover leaf. You carry
the landing gear's click and the engine's roar.
The bop of the ball, the shouts of soccer
in every dialect (*this is Queens*). You carry
the Vesper Sparrow, Rock Pigeon, American Wigeon,
Least Sandpiper, Solitary Sandpiper, Laughing Gull,
Chimney Swift, Ovenbird, Bufflehead,
Forster's Tern, Mute Swan, Ruddy Turnstone—
and the Common Grackle. As well as
charcoal and barbecued meats. And, hats.
(Bring back my hat!)

Oda al Aire del Prado Flushing/Parque Corona
por Kimiko Hahn

Enmarcado por el Van Wyck, el Gran Central,
Union Turnpike, y el Lago Meadow--
giras y enfrías. Te abres a todxs
en cada clima. Llevas humos de escape
y zumbido de tráfico sobre hoja de trébol. Llevas
el clic del equipo de aterrizaje y el clamor del motor.
El golpeo de la bola, los gritos de fútbol
en cada dialecto (¡es Queens!). Llevas
la gorriona víspera, el pichón, el pato silbón,
los andarrios, la gaviota sonriente
el vencejo, la curruca, el pato Bufflehead,
el charrán de Forster, el cisne mudo, el vuelvepiedra
rubicunda--y el grackle común. Tanto como
carbon y la parillada. Y sombreros.
(¡Devuelveme mi sombrero!)

☼

法拉盛草甸科罗娜公园的空气颂
吉米柯 · 哈恩

在范威克高速公路、中央高速公路、联邦收费高速公路
和草甸湖的映照下，你飘来飘去，浑身冰凉。
你在任何天气都对一切开放，
你带着车流的尾气和嗡嗡声
穿过一片三叶草叶。
你带着起落架的咔哒声和发动机的轰鸣声。
足球的波普声，每种方言的
足球观众呐喊声（这是皇后区）。
你载着晚祷麻雀，岩鸽，绿眉鸭，
最小的矶鹬，孤独的矶鹬，笑鸥，
北美燕子，橙顶灶莺，白枕鹊鸭，
福斯特燕鸥，疣鼻天鹅，赤翻石鹬——
还有拟八哥。以及带着木炭和烤肉。
还载着帽子。（把我的帽子带回来！）

Ode to the Mud in Flushing Meadows Corona Park
by Kimiko Hahn

"Walk so silently that that the bottoms of your feet become ears."
—*Pauline Oliveros*

After all, you persist this late winter
to offer history and souvenir—
so I walk—as a teacher instructed—
listening to you with my feet. I hear
the slow creak of a glacier, ice sheets
breaking stone into terminal moraine.
I hear the waters in a glacial lake and rivulets.
Torrents turning earth to marsh.
Then, the Lanape hunted then the Dutch
used tufts and such for grazing animals.
I hear their lowing. I hear muskets.
I hear the metal on road and rail.
And after the rich enjoyed a quiet green resort,
there came dumping. Can you hear the tons
of ash? Can you hear the stench and infestation?
Can you hear the fur trappers and squatters?
I hear them and the locals collecting firewood.
I hear the lawns unrolled for the fair.
The vigils and games! (The crimes—
we can't forget the crimes—)
Hear the picnic benches and picnickers.
Hear the macadam. The gravel. Hear
new stampedes. New trains of thought.
New embraces. New loves.
I listen to you whispering to my feet.

Oda al Fango del Prado Flushing/Parque Corona
por Kimiko Hahn

"Camina tan silenciosamente que la planta de tus pies se vulve oidos."

--Pauline Oliveros

Despues de todo, persistes en este invierno tarde
para ofrecer historia y recuerdo--
asique camino--como maestra enseñada--
escuchándote con mis pies. Oigo
el crujido lento de un glaciar, hojas de hielo
rompiendo piedra, convirtiéndola en escombros terminal.
Escucho las aguas en un lago glacial y riachuelos.
Torrentes haciendo tierra pantano.
En esos dias, los Lanape cazaban, y los Holandés
usaban mechones de hierba para apacentar animales.
Oigo sus mugidos. Oigo los mosquetes.
Oigo el metal en la carretera y el carril.
Y despues que los ricos han disfrutado
un complejo tranquilo y verde,
vino el basurero. ¿Puedes oir los montones
de ceniza? ¿Puedes oir el hedor y infestación?
¿Puedes oir el cazador de pieles y el squatter?
Oigo a ellos y los indigenas recogiendo leña.
Escucho el césped desenrollado para la feria.
¡Las vigilias y los juegos! (Los crímenes--
no podemos olvidar los crímenes--)
Escucha los bancos de picnic y los visitantes.
Escucha el cemento. La grava. Escucha
estampidas nuevas. Nuevos trenes de pensamiento.
Nuevos abrazos. Nuevos amores.
Te oigo susurrando a mis pies.

法拉盛草甸科罗娜公园的淤泥颂
吉米柯 · 哈恩

——波琳 · 奥利弗罗斯："静静地走，让你的脚底变成耳朵。"

毕竟，你坚持在这个冬末
提供历史和纪念品——
所以我按照老师的指示走路——
用脚听你说话。
我听到冰川缓慢的吱吱声，
冰盖将石头碎成冰碛。
我听到冰川湖和小溪中的水声。
洪流将地面变成沼泽。
然后，拉纳佩人开始狩猎，
然后荷兰人用簇绒等来放养动物。
我听到了它们的叫声，听到了滑膛枪声。
我听到了公路和铁路上的金属声。
富人在享受了一个安静的绿色度假胜地后，
随之而来的是倾倒垃圾。
你能听到倾倒成吨的灰烬声吗？
你能听到恶臭的害虫群袭吗？
你能听到捕猎者和非法占用者的声音吗？
我听到他们和当地人捡柴火的声音。
我听见草坪在为集市铺开的声音。
守夜和游戏！（犯罪-
我们不能忘记这些罪行——）
听到野餐长椅和野餐者的声音。
听到碎石声，砾石声。 听到
新的踩踏声。听到新的思路，
新的拥抱， 新的爱。
我听到你在我脚边耳语。

Poets' Biographies

Grisel Y. Acosta is a full professor at the City University of New York-BCC, and Creative Writing Editor at *Chicana/Latina Studies Journal*. Her book, *Things to Pack on the Way to Everywhere* (Get Fresh, 2021), was a 2020 finalist for the Andrés Montoya Poetry Prize. Select work is in *Best American Poetry, The Baffler, Acentos Review, Platform Review, NOMBONO: Speculative Poetry by BIPOC Poets,* and *The Future of Black: Afrofuturism, Black Comics, and Superhero Poetry.*

Kelli Russell Agodon's most recent book is *Dialogues with Rising Tides* (Copper Canyon Press, 2021). She is the cofounder, editor, and book cover designer at Two Sylvias Press. She lives in Washington on traditional lands of the Chimacum, Coast Salish, S'Klallam, and Suquamish people where she is an avid paddleboarder and hiker. She teaches at Pacific Lutheran University's low-res MFA program, the Rainier Writing Workshop.   agodon.com   twosylviaspress.com

Kim Barnes was raised in the logging camps and small towns of northern Idaho. Her books have been named among the best of the year by *San Francisco Chronicle, The Seattle Times, The Washington Post,* and *The Kansas City Star.* She is recipient of the PEN Center USA Award for Fiction as well as the PEN/Jerard Award for her memoir, *In the Wilderness,* which was also a finalist for the Pulitzer Prize. kimbarnes.com

Traci Brimhall is the author of: *Come the Slumberless from the Land of Nod* (Copper Canyon Press), *Saudade* (Copper Canyon Press), *Our Lady of the Ruins* (W.W. Norton), and *Rookery* (Southern Illinois University Press). Her poems have appeared in *The New Yorker, Poetry, Slate, The Believer, The New Republic, Orion, New York Times Magazine,* and *Best American Poetry.* She's received a National Endowment for the Arts Literature Fellowship and is currently Director of Creative Writing at Kansas State University.

Scott Chaskey is a poet, farmer, and educator. For 30 years he cultivated crops and community at Quail Hill Farm, Amagansett, N.Y., one of the original CSA's in the country. Past President of NOFA-NY, he was honored as Farmer-of-the Year in 2013, and has served as founding Board member for three land equity and social justice not-for-profits.

Author of *This Common Ground* (Viking), *Seedtime* (Rodale), *Stars are Suns*, *Soil and Spirit*, will be published by Milkweed Editions in 2023.

Dan Close is a poet and novelist living in northwest Vermont. He is the author of *What the Abenaki Say About Dogs*, a book of poetry which chronicles the lives of the Abenaki of the Champlain Basin. His novel, *The Glory of the Kings*, was awarded Best In Fiction by Peace Corps Writers. He is a member of the Poetry Society of Vermont. danclose.net

Ann Bemis Day started writing about nature in the early grades. She and her husband Frank Day's farm was the first property conserved by the Vermont Land Trust. Ann continues to work on conservation and writes a nature column for the *Valley Reporter* in Waitsfield VT. She has published several books of poetry and farming and caring for the land. Ann now lives in the Monadnock area where she writes poetry and articles on nature and fights for preserving land.

Kimiko Hahn is the author of ten books of poetry, including *Foreign Bodies* (W.W. Norton, 2020). She is a distinguished professor in the MFA Program in Creative Writing & Literary Translation at Queens College, City University of New York.

Lori Landau (she, her) is an interdisciplinary artist. She holds an MFA in Interdisciplinary Arts with a concentration in Decolonial Arts Praxis. Her deep engagement with lakes, birds, grasses, and seas source her eco-ethics. Her work is grounded in contemplative practices, poetics and training in compassionate integrity. Her writing can be found in a variety of magazines, anthologies and blogs, and her art has been shown on both coasts.

DJ Lee is a writer, scholar, artist, and regents professor of English at Washington State University. She has published over forty essays and prose poems, the memoir *Remote: Finding Home in the Bitterroots* (Oregon State 2020), and eight scholarly books, including *The Land Speaks* (Oxford 2017). A hand papermaker and photographer, Lee often combines image and text. Artist residencies include the Arctic Circle Artist Residency, Women's Studio Workshop, and the Wilderness Art Collective.

Joanna Suzanne Lee is the author of *Dissections* (2017), a co-editor of the anthology *Lingering in the Margins* (2019), and founder of the Richmond, Virginia community River City Poets. Her work has been published or is forthcoming in *Rattle, Fourth River, Driftwood* and elsewhere, and has been nominated for both Best of the Net and Pushcart prizes.

JuPong Lin, an immigrant from Taiwan, weaves her ancestral traditions into community performances, cultivating kinship between humans of different places and with our more-than-human kin. As an artist, de/colonial and institutional activist and educator, she fuses story circle, qigong, and cultural somatics in a relational art that bridges personal and collective healing. JuPong currently chairs the MFA in Interdisciplinary Arts program at Goddard College.

Jesse LoVasco, (she/her) is a poet, visual artist and herbalist, residing in occupied land of Anishnabe in Michigan and occupied land of Abenaki in Vermont. Her poems appeared in *Written River* of Hiraeth Press 2012, *the Sea Letter* and *Literary North*. Her first online chapbook, was published with Red Wolf Editions, an online publisher, entitled *Imprinting Waves*, in 2018. And she is the winner of the Homebound Publications Poetry Prize 2019- published 2020, entitled *Native*.

Denise Low, Kansas Poet Laureate 2007-09, is winner of a Red Mountain Press Award for *Shadow Light*. Other publications include: *The Turtle's Beating Heart: One Family's Story of Lenape Survival* (U. of Nebraska Press), a Hefner Heitz Award finalist; *Wing* (Red Mountain); *Casino Bestiary* (Spartan); and *Jackalope* (Red Mountain, fiction). At Haskell Indian Nations University she founded the creative writing program. deniselow.net

Maiah A Merino, a Chicanx Poet and mixed-genre writer, recently co-edited The Yellow Medicine Review's Spring 2022 Journal: *Miracles & Defining Moments*. She has poems in *In Xóxitl, in cuícatl: Flor y Canto, Antología de poesía,* an international bilingual poetry anthology. A recipient of the 2021 Artist Trust GAP Award, her work appears in *The Yellow Medicine Review,* and *The Raven Chronicles.* She is a past Writer-in-Residence with Seattle Arts and Lectures, and Path with Art.

Caryn Mirriam-Goldberg, Ph.D., Kansas Poet Laureate Emerta, is the author of 24 books, including *How Time Moves: New & Selected Poems; Miriam's Well,* a novel; *Needle in the Bone,* a non-fiction book on the Holocaust; and *The Sky Begins At Your Feet.* Founder of Transformative Language Arts, she coaches people on writing and right livelihood. She lives in Kansas on a conservative easement she and her husband steward. CarynMirriamGoldberg.com YourRightLivelihood.com Bravevoice.com

Dr. Gwyn R. C. Moses's titles include *A Perfect Fit, My Teacher Made Me Write This, Bees and Butterflies, Tapped, Reflections: Connect with God, Down by The Riverside, Olive Grey, Myracle's Hope: A Ticket to African American History,* and *SHE, Fully Hydrated.* She is featured in *Virginia Bards Central Review Poetry Anthology 2019,* and authors a Podcast "Nature Amends," & hosts YouTube Candid Conversations with Author Gwyn R.C. Moses.

Ryan Victor Pierce or **"Opalanietet"** (Nanticoke Lenni-Lenape) has performed at New York City Opera at Lincoln Center, Ashtar Theater in Palestine, and gave the first-ever Lenape Land Acknowledgement at the Macy's Thanksgiving Day Parade on NBC. He is also the Founder of Eagle Project. Opalanietet is currently studying for his doctorate in Theatre & Performance at the City University of New York (CUNY) Graduate Center. eagleprojectarts.org

Rachelle Parker is a Nassawadox born, Brooklyn bred writer. Her forthcoming, debut collection *Together We Remember The Gazelle* was selected poetry winner of the 2022 Digging Press Chapbook Series. She is a resident of Storyknife Writers Retreat: A women writers retreat in Homer, Alaska.   linktr.ee/RachelleParkerWriter.

Laurel S. Peterson has published work in in many literary journals and has two poetry chapbooks as well as two full-length collections, *Do You Expect Your Art to Answer?* and *Daughter of Sky,* both from Futurecycle Press. She also wrote two mystery novels, *Shadow Notes* and *The Fallen* (Woodhall 2021). She is on the editorial board of the literary magazine *Inkwell,* and served as the town of Norwalk, Connecticut's, Poet Laureate from April 2016 – April 2019.

Michaeline Picaro is a member of the Ramapough Lunape Nation Turtle Clan and a co-founder of the Munsee Three Sisters Medicinal Farm and of Ramapough Culture and Land Foundation; Preserving and restoring the economic, social, cultural, sacred and environmental assets of the Ramapough Munsee ancestral lands. She is Tribal Historic Preservation Officer for Turtle Clan, Ramapough Lenape Nation, and a preservationist for sacred ceremonial landscapes.

Maria Elena Scott is a graduate of UW-Madison, Wisconsin currently living in Richmond, Virginia. She is a member of James River Writers and River City Poets, and is published in *Yellow Medicine Review-A journal of Indigenous Literature, Art and Thought* (Spring 2019) and (Fall 2019) editions. An essay "English Only Has Twenty-Six letters" was published in *South Florida Poetry Journal*, February 2021. Her self-published memoir is titled: *A Love Letter To My Brother Juan* (2022).

Dorinda Wegener is Co-founder of Trio House Press. Her work appears in many journals, including *The Antioch Review, Indiana Review, Hotel Amerika, THRUSH, Berkeley Poetry Review,* and *Hinchas de Posia,* as well as anthologized within *Poet Showcase: An Anthology of New Hampshire Poets* (Hobblebush Books) and *Lingering in the Margins: A River City Poets Anthology* (Chop Suey Books). Dorinda currently works as a Registered Nurse, she wants you to wear a mask and get vaccinated.

Robert Wrigley was born in Illinois and has lived in Montana, Washington, Oregon, and mostly Idaho, for forty-five years. He has published eleven books of poems and one collection of essays, *Nemerov's Door. The True Account of Myself as a Bird,* will appear from Penguin in June, 2022. He is the recipient of two NEA Fellowships and a Guggenheim Foundation Fellowship. He lives in the woods a few miles from Moscow, Idaho.

Artists' Essayists', and Translators' Biographies

Grisel Y. Acosta is a full professor at the City University of New York-BCC, and Creative Writing Editor at *Chicana/Latina Studies Journal*. Her book, *Things to Pack on the Way to Everywhere* (Get Fresh, 2021), was a 2020 finalist for the Andrés Montoya Poetry Prize. Select work is in *Best American Poetry, The Baffler, Acentos Review, Platform Review, NOMBONO: Speculative Poetry by BIPOC Poets*, and *The Future of Black: Afrofuturism, Black Comics, and Superhero Poetry*.

Tricia Bohan has lived in Branford, CT for most of her life, photographing and enjoying the beauty that surrounds us for the past 40+ years. The marshlands are always where she sees the most beauty and wildlife all year long.   tricia@tbphoto.com

Martin Bridge (cover artist) Martin's work spans a wide range of media from Drawing, Painting, Sculpture, Theater Design and Site Specific Installations to Performance. He bridges realms of science and mysticism in an effort to challenge the cultural paradigms that dictate how we relate to both the natural world as well as to our brothers and sisters. thebridgebrothers.com   patreon.com/martinclarkbridge

Lauren Brown is the author of two botanical field guides: *Weeds and Wildflowers in Winter* (WW Norton) and *Grasses, Sedges, Rushes: An Identification Guide* (Yale University Press). She has been involved for many years with the Branford Land Trust.

Rex Buchanan grew up in Kansas, on the edge of the Smoky Hills. He has degrees from Kansas Wesleyan University and the University of Wisconsin-Madison. After 38 years at the Kansas Geological Survey at the University of Kansas, he retired as Director Emeritus in 2016. He is the co-author of *Petroglyphs of the Kansas Smoky Hills* and *Roadside Kansas: A Traveler's Guide to Its Geology and Landmarks*, and editor of *Kansas Geology: An Introduction to Landscapes, Rocks, Minerals, and Fossils*.

Gerry Casanova is a Branford (CT)-based artist whose work across a variety of media aims to dramatize or reinterpret beauty found in common objects and settings.

Chen Yihai 义海 is a bilingual poet, and a professor in Yancheng Teachers University, Jiangsu Province, China. He has published approximately 30 books. His publications include translations of Western classics and his own poetry collections. His translations include *Pride and Prejudice, Robinson Crusoe*, Sara Teasdale's poems and Johnny Gruelle's children books. He has been awarded twice the highest literary prize "Zijinshan Prize" of Jiangsu Province, one for poetry, one for prose.

Jan Doyle I love photography. I incorporate my images into presentations that I present throughout the United States. As a quilt artist, photos provide the inspiration for my Thread Painting Quilts wyseworks.net

Silvia Drewery is a watercolourist who paints in the studio or en plein air. The marshlands of Branford (CT) and its wildlife have often been the subject of her paintings.

Barbara Dwyer is a photographer local to Branford, CT who loves exploring the many trails, woods, and land trust preserves in this part of the state. Nature, the landscape, and the intricacies of light and shadow are what compel her to pursue her art.

Marty Espinola I am a retired school teacher and administrator. These days I spend as much time as I can outdoors as I search for the endless variety of compositions that nature provides. Through photography I try to reproduce visually the beauty that I encounter in the world around me and to share that with others. I hope my images express my appreciation as well as my emotional response to what comes my way.

Lisa Hesselgrave's work centers on figures, landscapes and the alchemy that occurs when the two subjects intersect. She lives in an old house, near the edge of the woods, where she produces images combining an adherence to craft with personal content.

Carol Cable Hurst grew up along the Connecticut shoreline where she has enjoyed drawing and painting for 86 years. She is a member of the Branford Land Trust. The Vedder Preserve is her favorite view in Branford.

Jerry Jost is the executive director of the Kansas Land Trust.

Trish Karter paints en plein air, alla prima, in oil, interpreting nature in the moment. Always seeking the remarkable light effects and embracing all weather and conditions, she finds connections between the beauty and power of nature and man's puzzling behavior as she tries to make sense of what's happening around her. Her work is a journey of experimentation and trying to see more clearly, more empathically. www.lighteffectstudio.com

Ryan Kegley lives amongst the tallgrass prairie just west of Manhattan, Kansas, where he spends his free time immersed in and inspired by the natural beauty of the Flint Hills.

Tim Lawson is a Jefferson Land Trust Board member, photographer, and woodworker residing in Port Townsend, Washington. He's a member of LEO (the League of Extraordinary Observers), lending his time and talent to photograph conservation projects throughout Jefferson County.

Katie McBride is an illustrator and designer in Richmond, VA. She has a particular interest in creating images that connect people to stories and experiences, especially those involving the natural world. She has taught art to kids and adults, and is on the board at Gallery5. katiemcbride.com

Jeanette Mobeck, lifelong Branford, CT resident married to Bob Mobeck, enjoyed a career in New Haven Public Schools as a Speech/Language Pathologist. Jeanette has actively painted for 20 years using various mediums. She is a board member of Branford Arts and Cultural Alliance.

Jerry Monkman is a conservation photographer, filmmaker, and writer. He has written ten books and directed a feature-length documentary film. He and his wife Marcy run Ecophotography. ecophotography.com

Brian Obermeyer is The Nature Conservancy's director of land protection and stewardship in Kansas. Brian works with ranchers, landowners and other stakeholders to help preserve the biological integrity of this impressive landscape. Brian holds a master's degree in environmental biology from Emporia State University. He has received awards from the Kansas Wildlife Federation and the National Association of Fish and Wildlife Agencies.

Sylvia Ohlrich is a photographer who enjoys nature while hiking trails and discovering beautiful places to photograph. Prior to shooting digital work she worked in analog in color and black and white.

Gaile Ramey trained in the lineages of sculptor Mark Di Suvero and luminary photographer Harry Callahan. She created the photography artbook, *Women are Perfect- Women's March on Washington 2017*. She has exhibited her art on the east coast.

Deirdre Baker Schiffer studied art at The Cooper Union and Indiana University and maintained a studio in New Haven. Her family life in Branford, CT centered on the Farm River which recalled her childhood in Old Lyme on the Connecticut River.

Maria Stockmal paints primarily in oil paint or oil pastel. In February and March 2022, two of her oil painting were on display at the Three Rivers Community College's new gallery opening. m.stockmal@snet.net

Robert Thomas is an artist who has documented his world since the mid-twentieth century. His themes are inspired by the landscapes, be they urban or rural, and the imagery captured in the beauty and fragility found in nature. bob@artistsimaging.com

Patty Towle is a collage artist inspired by nature—birds, animals, plants, and healthy habitats. She uses cut paper, found papers and objects, photographs, and multimedia to translate nature's beauty to images.

Dr. Stephen C. Trombulak is Professor Emeritus of Biology and Environmental Studies at Middlebury College in Vermont. He holds a B.A. in Biology from UCLA and a Ph.D. in Zoology from the University of Washington. He joined the Middlebury College faculty in 1985, teaching and conducting research in environmental science, sustainability studies, natural history, and conservation biology. Most recently he was co-editor of the book *Landscape-scale Conservation Planning*.

Sarah Welch is an ecology-based educator, artist, and writer. As Hilltown Land Trust's 2021-2022 TerraCorps Community Engagement Coordinator, Sarah supports HLT's outreach and programming efforts. She holds an MS in Environmental Studies from Antioch University New England. sarah@hilltownlandtrust.org

Zhang Ziqing 张子清 , Professor of Institute of Foreign Literature, Nanjing University, Nanjing. Publications include *Two Sides of the Globe: Contemporary Chinese and American Literatures and Their Comparison*; *A History of 20th Century American Poetry*, and *On American New Pastoral Poems*. Translations span from *Selected Poems from T. S. Eliot* (1985), to *Always A Reckoning And Other Poems by Jimmy Carter* (2006). His work has received many honors and awards in China and the US.